BATTLE TANKS
AND SUPPORT VEHICLES

GREENHILL MILITARY MANUALS

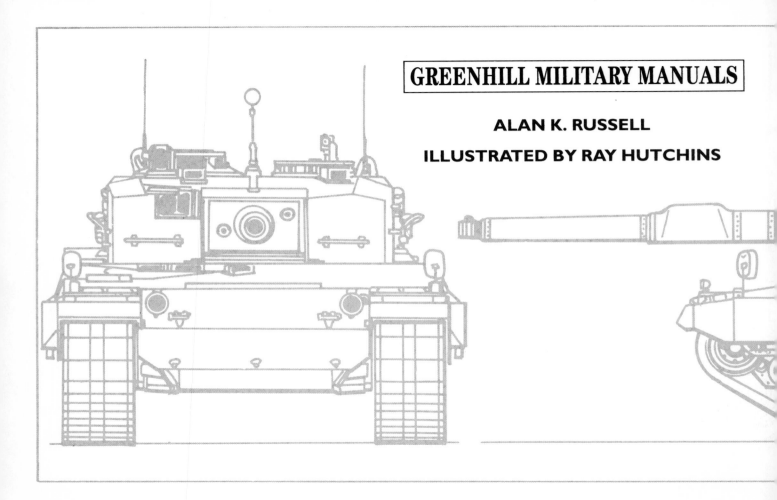

GREENHILL MILITARY MANUALS

ALAN K. RUSSELL

ILLUSTRATED BY RAY HUTCHINS

BATTLE TANKS
AND SUPPORT VEHICLES

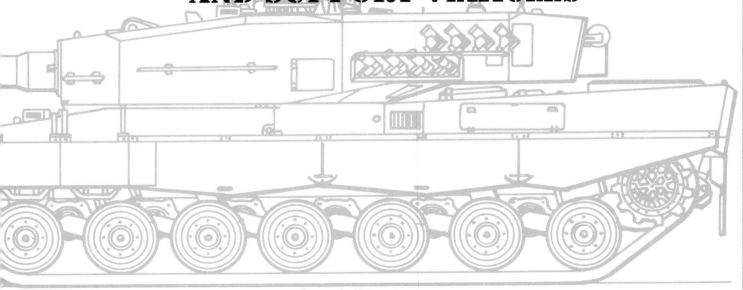

Greenhill Books, London
Stackpole Books, Pennsylvania

Battle Tanks and Support Vehicles
first published 1994 by
Greenhill Books, Lionel Leventhal Limited, Park House,
1 Russell Gardens, London NW11 9NN
and
Stackpole Books, 5067 Ritter Road, Mechanicsburg, PA 117055, USA

British Library Cataloguing in Publication Data
Russell, Alan K.
Battle Tanks: and Support Vehicles – (Greenhill Military Manuals)
I. Title   II. Series   623.7
ISBN 1-85367-174-6

Library of Congress Cataloging-in-Publication Data
Russell, Alan K.
Battle tanks and support vehicles/by Alan K. Russell.
p. cm. – (Greenhill military manuals)
ISBN 1-85367-174-6 (hc) : $19.95
1. Tanks (Military science) – Handbook, manuals, etc.
2. Vehicles, Military – Handbooks, manuals, etc.
I. Title.   II. Series.
UG446.5.R73 1994   93-36814
358.1'883-dc20   CIP

Typeset by Merlin Publications
Printed and bound in Great Britain by
Butler & Tanner Ltd, Frome and London

Introduction

Over the past twenty years the Main Battle Tank has regained its place as the 'Queen of the Battlefield' by virtue of a series of technological revolutions in the field of passive and active armour protection. Threatened almost to the point of battlefield extinction by the advent of multitudes of light anti-armour infantry weapons and various anti-tank guided missiles, all of which can easily punch holes through large thicknesses of conventional homogenous steel armour plate. The world's major tank designers fought back with what was originally considered to be unconventional ideas but are now accepted universally.

In the West the breakthrough was considered to be the UK's development in the sixties (with fielding in the early eighties) of the layered composite 'Chobham' armour. An effort which has been matched by America's development of its even more advanced 'Depleted Uranium' heavy armour package for the M1 Abrams MBT family; whilst in Israel and the East it was the development and use of 'reactive' armour blocks used to disrupt shaped-charge warheads. All these concepts set back the anti-tank weapon designers for years until new methods of penetrating the armour protection such as tandem warheads, precursor charges etc. could be developed to redress the balance somewhat.

Also of growing concern to the major powers is the acquisition of indigenous MBT design and manufacturing capabilities by what are now being termed 'Regional Superpowers'. With sufficient battle experience and the necessary infrastructure, like Iraq had for the Second Gulf War against the UN Coalition forces, these powers can easily challenge on the regional level with a good chance of creating significant regional conflicts.

The Conventional Forces Europe (CFE) talks have reduced the East/West European theatre tank forces to levels where such a scenario cannot be far removed from happening on a regular basis, especially with the thousands of spare MBTs which have become available for sale to any country which has the necessary hard cash available.

For the future, as the cost of the MBT rises, the need of the major powers is perceived as being for smaller numbers of higher quality vehicles. The UK's Challenger 2, France's Leclerc and America's M1A2 Abrams are typical examples of this philosophy. However, in order to afford these vehicles and keep an affordable national tank production capability it is vitally important for costs to be spread out. The only viable way for this to happen is for the vehicle to become an export item to valued client nations. It is therefore interesting to note that all three of these vehicles have had important export orders placed in the early nineties by such countries in the Middle East. How long can this continue is anybody's guess but a major reshaping of the world's MBT industries for the 21st Century is inevitable.

The Future

For the foreseeable future the main Western Powers, comprising the United States, France, Germany and the United Kingdom, will be periodically locked in battle to see which of their MBT designs will ultimately become the best seller on the world markets. Although sales are necessarily limited to those countries which can afford these vehicles, billions of pounds in export sales, the domestic capability to produce heavy armour and the national prestige associated with such sales are all at stake each time a tank competition is fought.

Recent experience has shown that the winner of a tank competition is not solely judged on the results of a single technical demonstration but rather either by the manufacturer that can offer the best industrial offset or, in some instances, for purely political reasons.

Of the four contending countries it is the United States General Dynamics M1A1/M1A2 Abrams that has tended to dominate the field with lucrative export sales to Egypt (M1A1), Kuwait (M1A2) and Saudi Arabia (M1A2). The Abrams battlefield performance in the Gulf War certainly helped its case with the latter two countries and these orders together with the US Army's programme to upgrade earlier M1 series tanks to the M1A2 standard has safeguarded US tank production into the next century.

The next in the league of four is France's Giat Industries Leclerc MBT. The recent United Arab Emirates order for a diesel engined version allowed a reasonable production level to be attained and confirmed Giat as one of Europe's major heavy armour producers.

Currently third in the league is Britain's Vickers Defence Systems Challenger 2. The winner of the British Army's MBT competition the production quantities required for the British Army and a single export order for Oman are not exactly awe inspiring. Unless further export orders or the British Army decides to re-equip with Challenger 2s then Vickers capacity in the longer as a MBT designer, developer and producer must be in some doubt.

Bottom of the list is Germany. Although the Krauss-Maffei Leopard 2 design has been sold to the Netherlands and Switzerland, and its Leopard 2 (Improved) version has been offered in competition with the Leclerc and M1A2 Abrams for Sweden's MBT requirement, stringent German export regulations are in force. These effectively mean that sales of the Leopard 2 to any non-NATO or non-European country are impossible.

It is highly likely that over the next decade or so the major Western heavy armour manufacturers are due for a major shake-up unless some major situation occurs that brings the manufacture of MBTs back as a matter of some priority. In the light of this it should be noted that the current trend towards reducing defence spending and the cutting of major defence programmes with the loss of strategic assets such as AFV manufacturers is definitely not good practice. Recent experience has shown that conflicts demand huge amounts of equipment and not politicians trying to balance the books. It only needs for a major industrialised country with worldwide commitments to be beaten once for the wolves to come knocking at the door to see what else is on offer.

General Dynamics M1A1.

Giat Industries Leclerc.

Vickers Defence Systems Challenger 2.

Krauss-Maffei Leopard 2.

Contents

Introduction 5

The Future..6

Contents..8/9

TAM (Tanque Mediano Argentino), Argentina 10

Bernadini MB-3 Tamoyo/Tamoyo III, Brazil 12

ENGESA EE-T1 OSORIO, Brazil 14

Type 59, People's Republic of China 16

Type 69/Type 79, People's Republic of China..............18

Type 80/Type 85/Type 90, People's Republic of China 20

T-55 AM, Czechoslovakia 22

GIAT Industries Leclerc, France 26

GIAT AMX-30/AMX-30 B2, France 32

Leopard 2/2A1/2A2/2A3/2A4/2A5 Series, Germany...34

Leopard 1/1A1/1A1A1/1A1A2/1A2/1A3 Series,
    Germany 38

Leopard 1A4/1A5/1A6 Series, Germany 40

Arjun Mk 1, India..42

Vijayanta, India 44

VFM 5 Vickers Defence Systems/FMC,International 48

T-55 variants, Iraq 50

Merkava Mk 3/Mk 4, Israel 52

Merkava Mk 1/Mk 2, Israel 54

Mag'ach (Upgraded M48/M60 series Patton), Israel 57

Sho't (Upgraded Centurion), Israel 59

M51 Isherman (M51 Sherman), Israel 61

OTO Melara/IVECO Fiat C-1 Ariete, Italy 63

OTO Melara OF40 Mk 1/Mk 2, Italy..............................65

Mitsubishi Type 90, Japan 68

Mitsubishi Type 74, Japan 70

Mitsubishi Type 61, Japan 72

Vickers Defence Systems Khalid, Jordan 74

TR-77 (export)/TR-580/TR-800 (export)/TR-350,
Romania 76

Olifant Mk 1A/Mk 1B, South Africa 78

K1 (Type 88 or ROKIT), South Korea 80

T-80 Series, former Soviet Union 83

T-72B/T-72S (export) series, former Soviet Union 86

T-72, A, G, M1 and PT-91 series, former Soviet Union 88

T-72, A, B (export) and M series, former Soviet Union ...90

T-64 series, former Soviet Union.....................................92

T-62 series, former Soviet Union.....................................95

T-55 series, former Soviet Union.....................................98

T-54, former Soviet Union 100

T-34-85, former Soviet Union 102

Bofors Stridsvagn (Strv) 103A/B/C, Sweden.................104

Pz68 series, Switzerland 106

Pz61 series, Switzerland 108

Vickers Defence Systems Challenger 2, UK.................110

Vickers Defence Systems Challenger 1, UK.................114

Vickers Defence Systems Chieftain FV4201/
Improved Chieftain FV4030/1, UK 120

Vickers Defence Systems Mk 1/Mk 3, UK 124

Centurion, UK..126

General Dynamics Abrams M1A1/M1A1 (HA)/
M1A2, USA..130

General Dynamics Basic Abrams M1/
Improved Performance M1, USA................................136

M60A3/M60A3 TTS Patton, USA..................................140

M60/M60A1 Patton, USA 144

M48A5 Patton, USA..148

M48A1/M48A2/M48A3 series Patton, USA 152

M47/M47M Patton, USA..155

M-84, former Yugoslavia 158

Abbreviations 160

TAM (Tanque Mediano Argentino)   Argentina

The **TAM** was designed by the West German firm of Thyssen Henschel to meet the requirements of the Argentinian Army. The contract also included a design requirement for an infantry combat vehicle model which was produced under the final designation **VCTP (Vehiculo de Combate Transporte de Personal)**.

Production of the conventionally armoured TAM medium tank commenced in Argentina in the late seventies but was curtailed in the early eighties because of the country's serious financial difficulties which ultimately caused approximately 30% of the tanks built to be put directly into war stowage reserve by the Argentinian Army.

The TAM chassis and powerpack system are based on those used in the Marder ICV. The main armament, however, is a two axis stabilised locally developed 105 mm rifled tank gun with bore evacuator and thermal sleeve. The gun fires all the NATO standard 105 mm ammunition types.

The fire control system is of the coincidence rangefinder sight type and is operated by the commander. The gunner and loader also have their observation sight systems. A night driving capability is provided.

A prototype conversion to an ARV variant, the **VCRT**, has been made but not produced. A self-propelled howitzer, the **VCA 155**, using an Italian made Palmaria type turret housing a 155 mm howitzer and a lengthened TAM Chassis has also been produced to the prototype stage with a number of turrets awaiting to be fitted. Other multiple rocket launcher carrier prototypes have also been produced but not taken to the production phase.

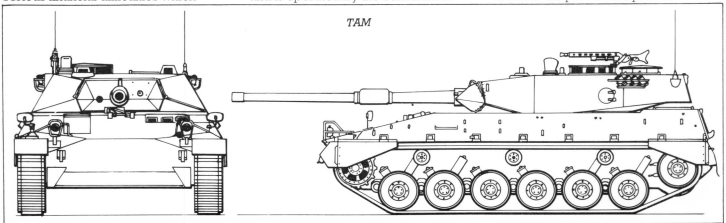

TAM

Thyssen Henschel has also built a private venture developmental follow-on to the **TAM** known as the **TH301** with an enhanced 750 hp rated powerpack, computerised fire control system with day/night thermal imaging observation and targeting system and a Rheinmetall 105 mm Rh 1055-30 rifled tank gun. To-date this has not been sold to any country.

Specification:
First prototype: ·1976
First production: 1979-85
(approx 350 built)
Current user: Argentina (including approx 1/3 in war reserve storage)
Crew: 4
Combat weight: 30 500 kg
Ground pressure: 0.77 kg/cm²
Length gun forwards: 8.23 m
Width: 3.12 m
Height (without AA gun): 2.42 m
Ground clearance: 0.44 m
Max. road speed: 75 km/h
Maximum range (with external fuel): 900 km
Fording: unprepared 1.4 m; prepared 4 m
Gradient: 60%
Side slope: 30%
Vertical obstacle: 0.9 m
Trench: 2.9 m
Powerpack: MTU MB 833 Ka-500 V-6 turbo-charged diesel developing 720 hp coupled to a Renk hydromechanical HSWL-204 transmission
Armament: (main) 1 x 105 mm gun (50 rounds); (coaxial) 1 x 7.62 mm MG; (anti-aircraft) 1 x 7.62 mm MG; (smoke dischargers) 2 x 4

TAM MBT of Argentinian Army.

Bernadini **MB-3 Tamoyo/Tamoyo III**   **Brazil**

The **Bernadini MB-3 Tamoyo** is in competition with the ENGESA EE-T1 Osorio design for a Brazilian Army requirement for approximately 500 MBTs.

Two versions of the MB-3 have been developed to-date.

MB-3 Tamoyo – initial model with MBT layout. It is armed with a 90 mm ENGESA EC90 series version of the Belgian Cockerill 90 mm rifled gun. The fire control system is of the computerised type with day/night sights fitted with integral laser range-finder modules for the commander and gunner. The standard equipment fit includes an NBC system and the armour protection on production vehicles will include special laminate and spaced armour types.

MB-3 Tamoyo III – upgraded version first seen in 1987 with new powerpack, spaced and special composite armour used in the hull and turret construction, an enhanced computer fire control system and a 105 mm Royal Ordnance L7A3 series rifled tank gun for which 50 rounds of ammunition is carried. The gun fires all the NATO standard 105 mm ammunition types.

An **ARV** and a **self-propelled anti-aircraft gun tank** are believed to be under development.

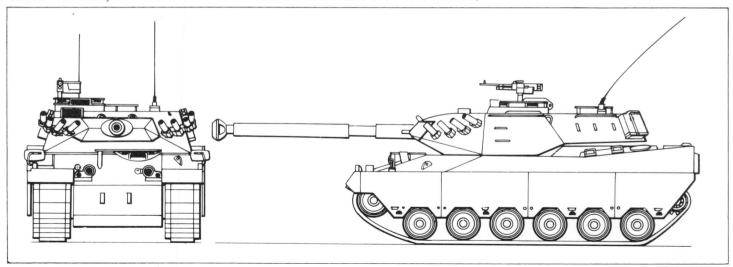

12

Specification:

First prototype: Tamoyo 1983; Tamoyo III 1987
First production: ready for production
Current user: none
Crew: 4
Combat weight: Tamoyo 30 000 kg; Tamoyo III 31 000 kg
Ground pressure: 0.72 kg/cm²
Length gun forwards: Tamoyo 8.8 m; Tamoyo III 8.9 m
Width (with skirts): 3.2 m
Height (without AA gun): Tamoyo 2.5 m; Tamoyo III 2.65 m
Max. road speed: 67 km/h
Maximum range: 550-600 km
Fording: unprepared 1.3 m
Gradient: 60%
Side slope: 30%
Vertical obstacle: 0.71 m
Trench: 2.4 m
Powerpack: Tamoyo – Saab – Scania DSI-14 diesel developing 500 hp coupled to an Allison CD-500-3 transmission; Tamoyo III – Detroit Diesel 8V-92TA developing 736 hp coupled to an Allison CD-850 series automatic transmission
Armament: (main) Tamoyo 1 x 90 mm gun (68 rounds), Tamoyo III 1 x 105 mm gun (50 rounds); (coaxial) 1 x 12.7 mm MG; (anti-aircraft) 1 x 7.62 mm MG; (smoke dischargers) 2 x 4

MB3 Tamoyo MBT with 90mm main gun.

ENGESA **EE-T1 OSORIO**   **Brazil**

The **EE-T1 OSORIO** was developed by the Brazilian company of ENGESA specifically for the export market using proven components wherever possible with Vickers Defence Systems of the United Kingdom being responsible for the complete turret. The EE-T1 OSORIO has been demonstrated in a number of countries in the Middle East but as of mid 1993 no firm orders had been placed. The Brazilian Army also has a requirement for a MBT and the two contenders for this are the EE-T1 OSORIO and the Bernardini MB-3 Tamoyo (qv).

Two basic versions of the ENGESA EE-T1 OSORIO have been developed to the protoype stage. The first of these, called the **EE-T1 P1** is armed with a British Royal Ordnance 105 mm L7A3 rifled tank gun and fitted with a computerised fire control system, day/night sights for commander and gunner with the latter having a laser rangefinder.

The second version (**EE-T1 P2**) has a French GIAT 120 mm smoothbore gun, a computerised fire control system, SFIM VS-580 model gyro-stabilised roof mounted sights for commander and gunner that incorporate laser rangefinders and a roof mounted Philips/TRT thermal imaging sight which can inject a picture into both the commanders and gunners sights. The customer can, however, select those systems which best meet his exact requirements.

The basic hull and turret of the EE-T1 OSORIO is of welded steel armour construction but over the frontal arc composite armour is used for increased battlefield survivability.

Standard equipment includes crew and engine compartment fire detection and suppression system, hydro-pneumatic suspension system developed by Dunlop of the UK, blow out panels in the roof of the turret bustle over the ready use ammunition stowage area and electric gun control equipment. A variety of options are available including auxiliary power unit (fitted to the second prototype), communications, land navigation system, laser detector system, NBC system and air conditioning system.

ENGESA has proposed that the chassis of the EE-T1 OSORIO can be used for a number of other applications including

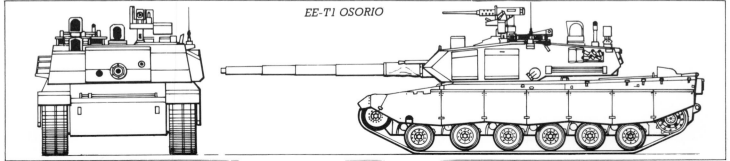

EE-T1 OSORIO

mounting various weapon systems, for example a twin 30/35 mm anti-aircraft turret, surface-to-air missile system and a 155 mm howitzer.

Specification:
First prototype: ·1984
First production: prototype stage
Current user: none
Crew: 4
Combat weight: EE-T1 P1 40 900 kg; EE-T1 P2 43 700 kg
Ground pressure: EE-T1 P1 0.72 kg/cm^2; EE-T1 P2 0.85 kg/cm^2

Length gun forwards: EE-T1 P1 9.4 m; EE-T1 P2 10.1 m
Width (with skirts): 3.26 m
Height (without AA gun): EE-T1 P1 2.7 m; EE-T1 P2 2.9 m
Ground clearance: 0.46 m
Max. road speed: 70 km/h
Maximum range: 500 km
Fording: 1.2 m
Gradient: 60%
Side slope: 30%
Vertical obstacle: 1.15 m
Trench: 3 m

Powerpack: MWM TBD 234 V-12 water-cooled turbocharged diesel developing 1100 hp coupled to ZF LSG 3000 automatic transmission
Armament: (main) EE-T1 P1 1 x 105 mm gun (45 rounds), EE-T1 P2 1 x 120 mm gun (38 rounds); (coaxial) 1 x 7.62 mm MG; (anti-aircraft) 1 x 12.7 mm MG; (smoke dischargers) 2 x 6

EE-T2 Osorio P2 prototype with 120 mm Giat Industries smoothbore gun.

Type 59   People's Republic of China

After the Soviet Union delivered a number of T-54 MBT in the mid fifties China subsequently produced the vehicle under the local designation **Type 59**. The major differences being in the adoption of a number of locally designed and built equipments such as fire control systems, etc. The 100 mm fired main gun is a copy of the Soviet D-10T tank gun with a total of 34 rounds carried for use. Most of the ammunition types used are direct copies of Soviet rounds but the China North Industries Corporation (NORINCO) is producing an indigenous 100 mm APFSDS-T round capable of effective engagements out to 2400 metres.

Over the years a number of variants have been identified. These are:

Type 59 Basic – believed similar to the T-54 Basic Model 1953, with most now upgraded to Type 59-I standard.

Type 59-I – similar to T-54A/B standard with a 100 mm gun fume extractor, active infra-red night fighting capability and, during the early eighties, the addition of a Yangzhou laser rangefinder module mounted over the main gun with matching improvements in the fire control system.

Type 59-II – a Type 59-I armed with a 105 mm rifled gun (Israeli in origin) that has the characteristic fume extractor and thermal sleeve of this weapon. NORINCO has developed its own 105 mm APFSDS-T round with an effective engagement range of 2500 metres.

Type 59R – A NORINCO conversion package for upgrading export Type 59/59-I models. It involves a new 730 hp diesel engine, the 100 mm APFSDS-T round, a new fire control system, full NBC protection and better running gear.

Type 59 ARV – the Type 59 Basic MBT converted to ARV towing configuration by removal of the turret.

The Pakistani Army has its own Type 59 rebuild facility, built with Chinese aid. This is now producing Type 69-II tanks and will eventually produce the MBT2000 design that has been co-developed with China

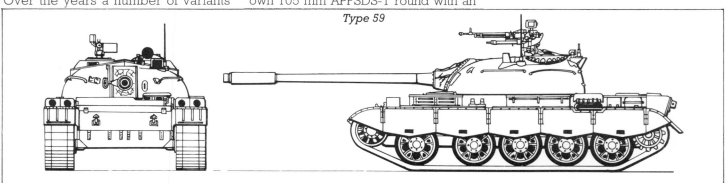

Type 59

Specification:
First prototype: 1956
First production: 1957-1987
Current users: Albania, Bangladesh, China, Congo, Cambodia, Iran, North Korea, Pakistan, Tanzania, Vietnam, Zimbabwe
Crew: 4
Combat weight: 36 000 kg
Ground pressure: 0.8 kg/cm^2
Length gun forwards: 9 m

Width: 3.27 m
Height (with AA gun): 2.59 m
Ground clearance: 0.43 m
Max. road speed: 50 km/h
Maximum range (with external tanks): 600 km
Fording: unprepared 1.4 m; prepared 5.5 m
Gradient: 60%
Side slope: 40%
Vertical obstacle: 0.8 m

Trench: 2.7 m
Powerpack: Model 12150L V-12 water-cooled diesel developing 520 hp coupled to a manual transmission
Armament: (main) 1 x 100 mm gun (Type 59 & Type 59-1) – 34 rounds), 1 x 105 mm (Type 59-II – 40 rounds); (coaxial) 1 x 7.62 mm MG; (bow) 1 x 7.62 mm MG; (anti-aircraft) 1 x 12.7 mm MG

Type 59 MBT.

Type 69/Type 79   People's Republic of China

The **Type 69** is an evolutionary development of the Type 59 to field new technology available in the armament, fire control system and night fighting equipment areas. The variants include:

Type 69 Basic – small number produced with 100 mm smoothbore main gun firing HVAPDS, HE-FS and HEAT-FS ammunition types, full NBC protection and night fighting capability.

Type 69-I – as for Type 69 Basic but addition of Yangzhou laser rangefinder module over main gun. Exported to Iraq.

Type 69-II – as for Type 69-I but with a 100 mm rifled main gun firing Chinese designed HEAT, HE, APHE and APFSDS rounds, new fire control system and side skirts. Exported to Iraq and Thailand. Iraq also modified some of its Type 69-II tanks with a stand-off armour package.

Type 69-IIB/Type 69-IIC – command tank versions with additional radios and second antenna on turret roof.

Type 69-IIC exported to Iraq.

Type 79 – Upgraded Type 69-II but with 105 mm rifled main gun, deletion of bow MG, modified turret with internal laser rangefinder and improved computer fire control system, new diesel powerpack installation and smoke discharger assemblies on either side of the turret.

Self-propelled AA guns – two twin 37 mm models, the **M1986** and **M1988** and the twin 57 mm **Type 80** vehicle.

Of which only the latter is in production. The Type 80 is the Chinese version of the Soviet ZSU-57-2.

Support vehicles – known types on the Type 69 chassis include the **Type 84 AVLB** and the **Type 653 ARV**.

Specification:

First prototype: ·Type 69 1967-68; Type 79 1979-80

First production: Type 69 1969-current; Pakistan (Type 69-II) 1991-current

Current users: (Type 69) China, Iran, Iraq, Pakistan, Thailand; (Type 79) China

Crew: 4

Combat weight: Type 69/Type 69-I 36 500 kg; Type 69-II 36 700 kg; Type 79 37 500 kg

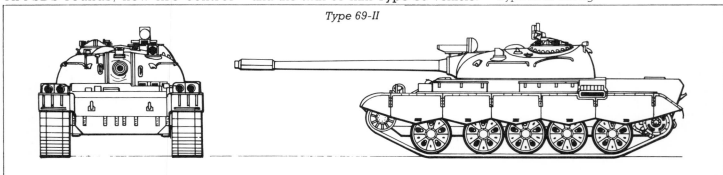

Type 69-II

Ground pressure: 0.82-85 kg/cm²
Length gun forwards: 8.68 m
Width (with skirts): 3.3 m
Height (with AA gun): 2.87 m
Ground clearance: 0.43 m
Max. road speed: Type 69 50 km/h; Type 79 60 km/h
Maximum range (with external tanks): Type 69 600 km; Type 79 520 km

Fording: unprepared 1.4 m; prepared 5.5 m
Gradient: 60%
Side slope: 40%
Vertical obstacle: 0.8 m
Trench: 2.7 m
Powerpack: Type 69 – Type 12150L V-12 liquid cooled diesel developing 580 hp coupled to a manual transmission; Type 79 – V-12 diesel developing 780 hp coupled to a manual transmission

Armament: (main) Type 69 1 x 100 mm gun, Type 79 1 x 105 mm gun; (coaxial) 1 x 7.62 mm MG; (bow) 1 x 7.62 mm MG (Type 69 only); (anti-aircraft) 1 x 12.7 mm MG; (smoke dischargers) 2 x 4 (Type 79)

Captured Type 69 MBT of Iraqi Army post Gulf War.

19

Type 80/Type 85/Type 90   People's Republic of China

The **Type 80** MBT is a further development of the Type 69-II design but with a 105 mm rifled main gun armament and matching NORINCO ISFCS-212 computerised fire control system. Rounds types carried include HEAT-T, HESH, APFSDS-T and HE ammunition types. An NBC protection system is fitted.

In the late eighties the **Type 85 MBT** is believed to have entered low rate production. This is based on the Type 80 chassis but with the first Chinese all welded turret instead of the normal cast steel type.

In 1991 the **Type 90-II** tank prototype was revealed. This in effect is the first new generation Chinese tank not drawing on the Type 59 design. It is armed with a Chinese version of the Russian 125 mm smoothbore gun design and autoloader assembly.

The variants identified to-date include the following:

Type 80-I – first production model.

Type 80-II – as Type 80-I but with new transmission, internal communications fit and a collective type instead of individual NBC defence system.

Type 85-II – essentially a Type 80-II but with new welded turret, 46 main gun rounds and different communications fit. Additional composite armour packages can be fitted to the hull and turret systems.

Type 85-II – as for Type 80-II but with only 44 rounds main gun ammunition and slightly different internal arrangement of turret systems.

Type 90-II – new generation tank with 125 mm gun, replaceable composite armour packages and fully computerised fire control system.

Specification:
First prototype: Type 80 1982; Type 85 1986; Type 90-II 1988-89
First production: Type 80 1984-current; Type 85 1987-current; Type 90-II none
Current user: China

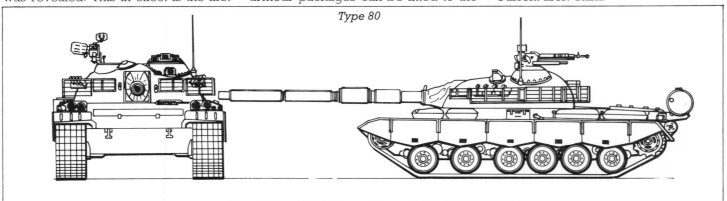
Type 80

Crew: 4
Combat weight: Type 80-I 38 000 kg; Type 80-11 38 500 kg; Type 85-II 39 000 kg; Type 85-IIA 39 500 kg; Type 90 48 000 kg
Ground pressure: n/av
Length gun forwards: Type 80-I 9.33 m Type 80-II 9.34 m; Type 85-II 9.34 m; Type 85-IIA 9.07 m; Type 90-II n/av
Width (with skirts): 3.37 m
Height (without AA gun): 2.3 m (2 m Type 90-II)
Ground clearance: 0.48 m
Max. road speed: 60 km/h
Maximum range (with external tanks): 570 km (400 km Type 90-II)
Fording: unprepared 1.4 m; prepared 5 m
Gradient: 60%**Side slope:** 40%
Vertical obstacle: 0.8 m
Trench: 2.7 m
Powerpack: Type 80 – V-12 diesel developing 730 hp coupled to a manual transmission; Type 80-II/Type 85-II/Type 85-IIA – same engine but with a semi-automatic transmission; Type 90-II – 6-cylinder diesel developing 1200 hp
Armament: (main) Type 80/85 – 1 x 105 mm gun (44 rounds Types 80, 80-II and 85-II, 46 rounds Type 85); Type 90-II – 1 x 125 mm gun (42 rounds); (coaxial) 1 x 7.62 mm MG; (anti-aircraft) 1 x 12.7 mm MG;(smoke dischargers) 2 x 4

Type 80 MBT with 105mm rifled gun main armament.

T-55AM   Former Czechoslovakia

In 1984 the the Czechoslovakian Army fielded an upgraded **T-55AM** version of the Soviet T-55 MBT. Designed to be the equivalent of the German Leopard 1A4, French AMX-30B2 or American M60A3, the **T-55AM** featured:-

i) an indigenously designed and built Kladivo fire control system which is characterised by a single wavelength laser rangefinder mounted above the main gun in an external container, a ballistic fire control computer, a wind velocity sensor and an armoured folding mast on the rear of the turret roof rear contains ambient temperature and air pressure sensors and a laser warning device to alert the tank crew if they are being lased by enemy tanks, aircraft, helicopters or artillery observers. With this fire control package the effective target engagement capability is increased from 1000 to 1600 metres.

ii) full track skirts which keep the dust down during vehicle movements and provide some additional armour side protection against light anti-tank weapons.

iii) metal side shields (horseshoe-shaped) of homogenus spaced armour on either side of the turret front for added protection against light anti-tank weapons

iv) a 250 m range smoke grenade launcher assembly which fires automatically if the laser warning device is

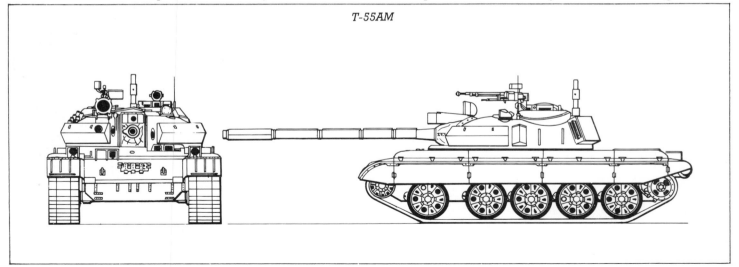

T-55AM

22

T-55AM with turret armour package.

T-55 AM – continued

activated to lay down a thermal sight defeating smoke screen.

v) additional armour on the glacis to improve protection against some SABOT round types and ATGW. The weight penalty is considerable and can affect vehicle handling if the engine has not been upgraded.

vi) improved engine and track suspension features to enhance cross-country mobility and offset increased vehicle weight

vii) thermal sleeve for the main armament.

Subsequently it was found that the modernisation programme had in fact been undertaken on a much wider scale in a number of the then Warsaw Pact nations and included a number of local variations. The modified T-54/T-55 vehicles serve with the Bulgarian, CIS, Hungarian, Polish and Russian armies. They were also used by the former East German army (including the AT-10 equipped Russian T-55AM2PB and Czechoslovakian T-55AM2B models).

Known variants of the **T-54/55** modernisation programme include:

T-54AM2 – Czechoslovakian Army rebuild of T-54 command tank with Kladivo fire control.

T-54AMK – Czechoslovakian Army rebuild of T-54K command tank with Kladivo fire control.

T-55AM – Czechoslovakian built T-55AM with Kladivo fire control system. Also used by Hungarian Army.

T-55AM1 – Czechoslovakian Army rebuild of T-55 with Kladivo fire control system. Also Russian T-55A(M) with laser rangefinder and armoured side skirts. Also used by Bulgarian Army. Also Polish Army rebuild of T-55 with locally developed Merida fire control system instead of the Klavido.

T-55AM2 – Russian T-55A(M) rebuild with full armour upgrade package, laser rangefinder and upgraded fire control system. Also used by Bulgarian Army. Also Czechoslovakian T-55 rebuild with Klavido fire control system and new engine.

T-55AM2B.– Czechoslovakian T-55 rebuild with full armour upgrade, Kladivo fire control system and integration of the AT-10 Stabber laser beam-riding ATGW with its associated 1K13 day/night sighting system.

T-55AM2P – Polish version of T-55AM2B using locally developed Merida fire control system in place of Klavido.

T-55AM2PB – Russian version of T-55AM2B using own Volna fire control system in place of Klavido.

T-55AM2K – Czechoslovakian T-55K commander's tank rebuild with Kladivo fire control system and new engine.

T-55MV – Russian T-55M upgraded with explosive reactive armour package.

T-55AMV – Further improved Russian T-55MV with the addition of a new commander's periscope, the use of T-72 running gear components and replacement of the 12.7 mm DShK AA machine gun by a 12.7 mm NSV model. The use of the ERA package increases the armour protection by 25% but adds another 1500 kg or so to the total combat weight.

NOTE: All the former Czechoslovakian Army modified T-54/55 tanks mentioned above are used by the Czech Republic and Slovakian Republic.

T-55AM with turret traversed to rear showing fire control meteorological sensor package on roof.

Specification:
First prototype: 1982-3
First production: approx 2200 conversions between 1984-1990 (in former Czechoslovakia alone)
Current users: Czech Republic, similar style conversions used by Bulgaria, CIS States, Hungary, Poland and Russia.
Crew: 4
Combat weight: 41 500 kg (T-55AM2B)
Ground pressure: n/av
Length gun forwards: 9.0 m
Width: 3.27 m
Height (without AA gun): 2.35 m
Ground clearance: 0.43 m
Max. road speed: 50 km/h
Maximum range (with external tanks): 650 km plus
Fording: unprepared 1.4 m; prepared 5.5 m
Gradient: 60%
Side slope: 30%
Vertical obstacle: 0.8 m
Trench: 2.7 m
Powerpack: upgraded V-12 water-cooled V-55 diesel coupled to a manual transmission
Armament: (main) 1 x 100 mm gun (42 rounds + 6 AT-10 ATGW); (coaxial) 1 x 7.62 mm MG; (anti-aircraft) 1 x 12.7 mm MG; (smoke dischargers) 1 x 8

GIAT Industries **Leclerc** **France**

The **GIAT Industries Leclerc** is France's third generation MBT replacement for the current AMX-30/AMX-30 B2 fleet. Apart from having the usual tank design characteristics of firepower, mobility and protection the **Leclerc** is introducing a fourth parameter to French tank construction – that of a real-time combat capability using a digital multiplex data bus to integrate the on-board electronic systems so as to allow automatic reconfiguration of the various pieces of equipment such as the fire control computer, gun-laying computer etc to overcome complete battlefield failure or damage.

The armour used in the hull and turret is of modular special armour ceramic composite and multi-layer steel types which provide a significant degree of frontal arc protection against KE as well as the more conventional anti-tank round types. The modularity allows for rapid package upgrading to meet new threats as they develop. Additional roof and belly armour protection is also provided against attack from those directions.

The main armament of the electric power operated turret is the GIAT Industries 120 mm smoothbore L52 tank gun with a Muzzle Reference System and a 22-round automatic loader system so as to reduce the turret crew number to two. The maximum effective rate of fire will be 12 rpm. The ammunition carried is of the APFSDS (with both tungsten and depleted uranium projectiles) and HEAT types with semi-combustible cartridges.

The latest generation gunner's, commander's and driver's day/night sights are incorporated in to the design. The gunner's SAGEM HL-60 and commander's SFIM HL-70 sights have integral passive thermal imaging and laser rangefinding capabilities with the former also having a built-in land navigation facility. These sights coupled with the digital data bus and computer fire control allows up to five targets per minute to be engaged compared to the three of current generation automatic computer fire control equipped tanks. First round hit

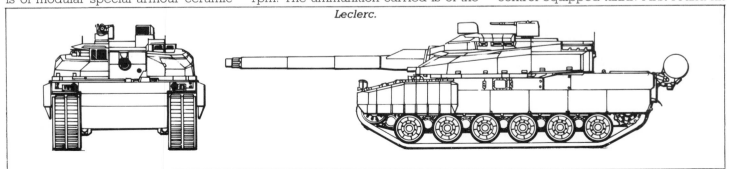

Leclerc.

A prototype Leclerc MBT.

Leclerc – continued

probability of a target at 2000 metres range with the **Leclerc** firing from the stationery position is over 80% whilst with it moving the same value is achieved at 1500 meters. A modern state-of-the-art NBC system is also carried.

The only combat support tank derivative announced to-date on the **Leclerc** chassis is an ARV, which GIAT Industries is developing as a private venture with Hagglund Vehicles of Sweden.

The total French Army requirement is for around 700 **Leclercs** but the figure has varied due to funding difficulties and new defence policies. The remainder of the estimated 1100 production **Leclercs** is taken up by the UAE (Abu Dhabi) order placed in early 1993 for 390 **Leclercs**. The MBT will differ from the standard French army model in being fitted with a German powerpack comprising an MTU MT-883 V-12 1500 hp diesel engine with a HSWL 295 automatic transmission. The UAE order also included 46 **Leclercs ARVs** and a comprehensive training (that included the provision of numerous simulators) and technical assistance packages to support the Leclerc fleet. Deliveries will be made in parallel to the production of the French Army vehicles.

A Leclerc MBT prototype on road test track.

Specification:

First prototype: 1989
First production: 1991-current (expected 1100 plus to be built)
Current users: France (also on order for UAE (Abu Dhabi) – 390 tanks)
Crew: 3
Combat weight: 53 500 kg
Ground pressure: 0.9 kg/cm²
Length gun forwards: 9.87 m
Width (with skirts): 3.71 m
Height (without AA gun): 2.46 m
Ground clearance: 0.5 m
Max. road speed: 73 km/h
Maximum range: 550 km
Fording: unprepared 1 m;
Gradient: 60%
Side slope: 30%
Vertical obstacle: 1.3 m
Trench: 3 m
Powerpack: SACEM UD V8X 1500 T9 Hyperbar 8-cylinder diesel developing 1500 hp coupled to an SESM ESM500 automatic transmission
Armament: (main) 1 x 120 mm gun (40 rounds); (coaxial) 1 x 12.7 mm MG; (anti-aircraft) 1 x 7.62 mm MG; (smoke dischargers) 2 x 9

One of the Leclerc MBT prototypes with turret traversed to right.

Leclerc MBT during cross- country trials.

Leclerc MBT at speed.

GIAT AMX-30/AMX-30 B2   France

The **GIAT AMX-30** series is currently the French Army's main MBT and will remain in service until it is superceded by the Leclerc.

A number of versions have been produced over the life time of the vehicle, these are:-

AMX-30 – the standard production model with a 105 mm GIAT CN-105-F1 rifled tank gun firing APFSDS, HEAT, HE smoke and illuminating rounds of both French and standard NATO M68/L7 patterns. The gunner has a coincidence rangefinder gun fire control system. For night fighting the vehicle has a white/infra-red search-light to the left of the main gun and infra-red night sights for the commander, gunner and driver. An NBC system is fitted as standard.

AMX-30S – optimised desert operation version of AMX-30 with downrated diesel to prevent overheating, side skirts and laser rangefinder unit for the vehicle commander.

AMX-30 B2 – both a new production and retrofit kit for significant portion of French Army AMX-30 vehicles and the export market. The changes include a new drive train gearbox system, modified gun mantlet with increased armour protection, the fitting of a fully integrated day/night computerised fire control system with laser rangefinder and LLLTV units and a collective NBC system.

The AMX-30 has also been the basis for a number of production combat support vehicles/weapon carriers, these include: the **AMX-30D ARV**, **AMX-30 AVLB**, **AMX-30 EBG** (equivalent to a CET), Pluton tactical nuclear battlefield support missile, Roland (for France, Iraq, Nigeria, Qatar and Spain) and Shahine (for Saudi Arabia) SAM missile systems, the 155 mm GCT self-propelled howitzer (for France, Iraq, Kuwait and Saudi Arabia) and the

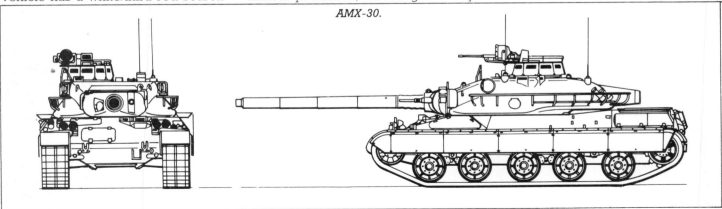

AMX-30.

AMX-30SA twin 30 mm self-propelled anti-aircraft gun tank (for Saudi Arabia).

The AMX-30 in its AMX-30S and AMX-30 B2 versions saw combat in the Gulf War with the French, Saudi Arabian and Qatari armies. The Qatari AMX-30S tanks being particularly effective in the retaking of Khafji when engaging Iraqi tanks.

Specification:
First prototype: 1960
First production: France 1966-current (2248 gun tank versions built to-date); Spain 1974-1983 (280 built)
Current users: Chile (AMX-30), Cyprus (AMX-30 B2), France (AMX-30/AMX30 B2), Greece (AMX-30), Qatar (AMX-30S), Saudi Arabia (AMX-30S), Spain (AMX-30E), UAE (AMX-30), Venezuela (AMX-30)
Crew: 4
Combat weight: AMX-30 36 000 kg; AMX-30 B2 37 000 kg
Ground pressure: AMX-30 0.77 kg/cm²; AMX-30 B2 0.85 kg/cm²
Length gun forwards: 9.48 m
Width: 3.1 m
Height (without AA gun): 2.29 m
Ground clearance: 0.44 m
Max. road speed: AMX-30/AMX-30 BS 65 km/h; AMX-30S 60 km/h
Maximum range: AMX-30/AMX-30S 500 km; AMX-30 B2 400 km

Fording: unprepared 1.3 m;
Gradient: 60%
Side slope: 30%
Vertical obstacle: 0.93 m
Trench: 2.9 m
Powerpack: AMX-30 – Hispano-Suiza HS110 multi-fuel V-12 liquid-cooled diesel developing 720 hp and coupled to a manual transmission; AMX-30S – as AMX-30 but diesel downrated to 600 hp for desert operations; AMX-30 B2 – as AMX-30 but HS-110-2 model diesel developing 700 hp
Armament: (main) 1 x 105 mm gun (47 rounds); (coaxial) 1 x 20 mm cannon or 12.7 mm or 7.62 mm MG; (anti-aircraft) 1 x 12.7 mm or 7.62 mm MG; (smoke dischargers) 2 x 2 or 2 x 4

French Army AMX-30B2.

Leopard 2/2A1/2A2/2A3/2A4/2A5 Series   Germany

The requirement for the **Leopard 2 MBT** grew out of the defunct American-German MBT-70 programme which took place in the late sixties. Krauss Maffei were contracted in the early seventies to build a series of prototypes armed with both 105 mm and 120 mm smoothbore tank guns. In 1977 the version fitted with a 120 mm gun and an advanced torsion bar suspension was selected for production as the Leopard 2. Subsequently a series of variants have been built:

Leopard 2 – 380 built with spaced composite armour construction of the turret and hull, 120 mm Rheinmetall smoothbore tank gun firing APFSDS-T and HEAT-MP-T projectiles with partially combustible cartridge cases.

A total of 42 120 mm rounds are carried with the gunner using a Krupp Atlas FLT-2/EMES-15 tank fire control system with full day/night sighting capability.

Leopard 2A1 – 750 built as for Leopard 2 but with integral thermal imaging sight. The Netherlands bought another 445 Leopard 2A1 modified to their own equipment standards under the designation Leopard 2NL.

Leopard 2A2 – the original 380 Leopard 2s remanufacturered to the Leopard 2A1 standard.

Leopard 2A3 – 300 built with minor internal/external changes.

Leopard 2A4 – 520 built in two batches with minor detail changes, updated fire control system and fitting of a crew bay

fire and explosion suppression system.

Leopard 2A5 – 175 built in two batches, further detail changes.

Pz 87 Leopard – Swiss Army version with first 35 built in Germany and delivered in 1987. The remaining 345 were built under license. Basically similar to German late production vehicles but to Swiss Army requirement fit standard (eg Swiss machine-guns, radios, etc).

Leopard 2 Driver Training Vehicle – a specialised driver training variant has been built on the Leopard 2 chassis. This has the regular turret replaced by an observation type fitted with a dummy main gun. A total of 22 have been bought by the German Army and 20 by the Netherlands.

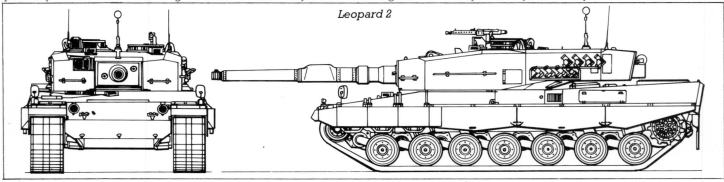

Leopard 2

Leopard 2 MBT.

Specification:
First prototype: 1972
First production: Germany 1978-1992
(2605 built); Switzerland 1987-1993 (total of
380 of which 345 license built)
Current user: Germany (see text),
Netherlands (Leopard 2NL), Switzerland
(Pz 87 Leopard)
Crew: 4
Combat weight: 55 150 kg

Ground pressure: 0.83 kg/cm²
Length gun forwards: 9.67 m
Width (with skirts): 3.7 m
Height (without AA gun): 2.79 m
Ground clearance: 0.49 m
Max. road speed: 72 km/h
Maximum range: 550 km
Fording: unprepared 1 m;
Gradient: 60%
Side slope: 30%

Vertical obstacle: 1.1 m
Trench: 3 m
Powerpack: MTU MB 837 ka-501 V-12
multi-fuel turbocharged diesel developing
1500 hp coupled to a Renk HSWL 354
automatic transmission
Armament: (main) 1 x 120 mm gun
(42 rounds); (coaxial) 1 x 7.62 mm MG;
(anti-aircraft) 1 x 7.62 mm MG; (smoke
dischargers) 2 x 8

Leopard 2 to 2A5 Series – continued

The Germany Army is to upgrade a number of its **Leopard 2** tanks to increase battlefield surviveability. This modification work includes the retro-fitting of additional special armour packages, the fitting of a new 120 mm L55 Rheinmetall gun and electric gun controls, upgrading of the sight and fire control systems to the latest state-of-the art. The upgraded version weighs around 62 000 kg and is know as the **Leopard 2 (Improved).** The programme is due to start in 1995 and finish in 2003.

The Dutch and Swiss are also due to upgrade their Leopard 2 tanks in a similar manner. The Dutch fleet of 445 at the same time as the Germans and the Swiss some 300 tanks from the year 2000 onwards.

In 1991 deliveries of an **ARV** versions, known as the **Buffel**, commenced to the German (75 vehicles) and Netherlands (25 vehicles) armies. The Buffel is fitted with the necessary rated hydraulic crane, winch, dozer blade and other equipment required to service or recover a Leopard 2 MBT.

Buffel ARV version of Leopard 2.

Leopard 2 during Swedish Army cold weather evaluation trials of tank.

Leopard 1/1A1/1A1A1/1A1A2/1A2/1A3 Series   Germany

The **Leopard 1** family grew out of the mid fifties agreement between France and West Germany to develop a common MBT design. In Germany the programme resulted in two competing design team vehicles series with the chosen vehicle design being approved for production in 1963. Since then a number of variants have been built, these are;

Leopard 1 – main production variant and armed with a Royal Ordnance 105 mm L7A3 rifled tank gun firing all NATO standard 105 mm tank gun ammunition types. The gunner has a TEM 2A stereoscopic rangefinder sight. The commander has his own TRP 2A sight. For night combat infra-red sighing and driving systems are used. There is also a dismountable white light/infra-red searchlight which can be fitted over the main gun.

Leopard 1A1 – refitted Leopard 1 with gun stabilisation system, thermal gun sleeve and new running gear components.

Leopard 1A1A1 – retrofitted Leopard 1A1 with special armour on turret sides and roof. Most of the vehicles are being upgraded to the Leopard 1A6 standard with a computerised fire control system and thermal imaging system for night fighting/poor visibility combat.

Leopard 1A1A2 – modified Leopard 1A1A1 with LLLTV observation and sighting system. Most vehicles are being upgraded to the Leopard 1A6 standard.

Leopard 1A2 – limited production model differing from Leopard 1A1 in only minor respects such as stronger turret, improved ventilation filters and the use of passive image intensifer night vision sights for the commander and driver.

Leopard 1A3 – limited production model as Leopard 1A2 model but built with new welded turret using all-round special spaced armour construction and other minor equipment modifications.

Combat support vehicles are dealt with in the Leopard 1A4/1A5/1A6 entry. By the mid-nineties the German Army will only have some 1200 odd Leopard 1's in service, mostly the latest versions.

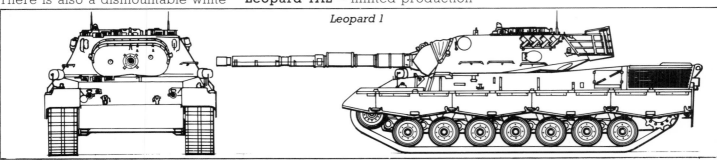

Leopard 1

Specification:

First prototype: ·1960
First production: Germany 1965-1984 (377 built by Krupp-MaK and Krauss Maffei), Italy 1974-83 (720 Leopard 1A2 license built by OTO Melara)
Current users: Australia (Leopard 1A3), Belgium (Leopard 1 being locally upgraded), Canada (Leopard 1A3), Denmark (Leopard 1A3), Germany (Leopard 1A1/1A1A1/1A1A2/1A2/1A3), Greece (Leopard 1A3), Italy (Leopard 1A2), Netherlands (Leopard 1 have been locally upgraded to Leopard 1-V standard equivalent to Leopard 1A1A1), Norway (Leopard 1 being locally upgraded to Leopard 1A5), Turkey (Leopard 1A1A1/1A3)
Crew: 4
Combat weight: Leopard 1 40 000 kg; Leopard 1A1/Leopard 1A1A1/Leopard 1A1A2 41 500 kg; Leopard 1A2/ Leopard 1A3 42 400 kg
Ground pressure: n/av
Length gun forwards: 9.54 m
Width (with skirts): 3.25 m
Height (without AA gun): Leopard 1 2.61 m; Leopard 1A1A1/1A1A2/1A2/1A3 2.74 m
Ground clearance: 0.44 m
Max. road speed: 65 km/h
Maximum range: 600 km
Fording: unprepared 2.25 m
Gradient: 60%
Side slope: 30%
Vertical obstacle: 1.2 m
Trench: 3 m
Powerpack: MTU MB 838 Ca M500 V-10 multi-fuel liquid-cooled diesel developing 830 hp coupled to a ZF 4 HP 250 transmission
Armament: (main) 1 x 105 mm gun (55 rounds); (coaxial) 1 x 7.62 mm MG; (anti-aircraft) 1 x 7.62 mm MG; (smoke dischargers) 2 x 4

Leopard 1 MBT with dismountable Whitelight/IR searchlight over main gun.

Leopard 1A4/1A5/1A6 Series   Germany

The **Leopard 1A4** was the last production model of the Leopard 1 series and is virtually the same as the Leopard 1A3 but with a computerised fire control system coupled to a fully stabilised main armament in place of the gunner's mechanically linked stereoscopic rangefinder sight. A total of 250 were built of which 150 have been transferred to Turkey as military aid, after modification to the new build Leopard 1A3 standard already in service with the Turkish Army.

In the early eighties West Germany trialled a number of computerised fire control systems in the Leopard 1 MBT for a proposed retrofit package. The system chosen was the EMES 18 and this, together with a passive thermal imaging night fighting system, was used from 1986 onward to upgrade 1300 Leopard 1A1A1 and Leopard 1A1A2 vehicles to the **Leopard 1A5** standard. However, this conversion turned out to be an interim standard as a further modification package was required to improve the tank's battlefield survivability factor by enhancing the armour protection with add-on armour and adding additional protection systems such as an explosion suppression unit to the turret area. All the 1300 tanks are to be converted to this standard which is designated the **Leopard 1A6**. A batch of 75 upgraded Leopard 1A5 tanks has been passed to Greece by the Germans.

A number of combat support vehicle types have either been built on or converted form the basic Leopard 1 chassis. These include the **Bergepanzer** and the **Product-improved Bergepanzer ARVs**, the **Pionierpanzer 1** and **Pionierpanzer 2 AEVs** and the **Biber AVLB**. There is also a tank dozer conversion kit used on the Leopard 1 (and Leopard 2) variants.

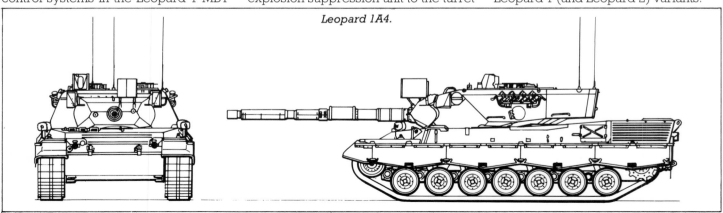

Leopard 1A4.

Specification:
First prototype: ·1960
First production: Leopard 1A4 1974-75 (250 built by Krupp MaK and Krauss Maffei); Leopard 1A6 1986-92 (1300 conversions by Wegmann from Leopard 1A1A1/1A1A2)
Current users: Germany (Leopard 1A4/1A5/1A6), Greece (Leopard 1A5), Turkey (Leopard 1A4 rebuilt to 1A3 Turkish Army standard)
Crew: 4

Combat weight: 42 400 kg
Ground pressure: 0.88 kg/cm^2
Max. road speed: 65 km/h
Length gun forwards: 9.54 m
Width (with skirts): 3.25 m
Height (without AA gun): 2.76 m
Ground clearance: 0.44 m
Maximum range: 450 km
Fording: unprepared 2.2 m
Gradient: 60%
Side slope: 30%
Vertical obstacle: 1.1 m

Trench: 2.9 m
Powerpack: MTU MB 838 Ca M500 V-10 multi-fuel liquid-cooled diesel developing 830 hp coupled to a ZF 4 HP 250 transmission
Armament: (main) 1 x 105 mm gun (55 rounds); (coaxial) 1 x 7.62 mm MG; (anti-aircraft) 1 x 7.62 mm MG; (smoke dischargers) 2 x 4

German Army Leopard 1A5.

Arjun Mk 1   India

The **Arjun** is India's first indigenous MBT design and has been developed by the Indian Army's Combat Vehicle Research and Developed Establishment (CVRDE) over a protected period from 1974 for an expected service entry in the early nineties. A total of 17 prototypes and 20 pre-production vehicles are being used in an extensive test and evaluation programme of all the various tank subsystems with the first pre-production series vehicle delivered in 1988. However, significant problems with the programme have resulted in major timescale overruns with the Arjun only just entering limited production. As an interim measure, license production of the Russian T-72M1 MBT was started in 1987. At present the cost of upgrading the various Indian tank fleets is slowing down the production rate even further so that the required number of Arjuns for ten tank regiments will not be met until around the year 2010.

Amongst the problems encountered is the design of a suitable local power-pack system thus the initial production batches will have to use an imported unit, the German MTU model used in some of the prototype vehicles.

The suspension is of the hydro-pneumatic type and the armour package type used is of a special composite type developed by the Indian Defence Metallurgical Laboratory.

The Arjun is armed with a locally designed stabilised 120 mm rifled gun firing similarly developed APFSDS, HEAT, HESH, HE and smoke round types. The associated fire control system is a full solution follow-on to the computerised Bharat Electronics Tank Fire Control System Mk 1B used on Vijayanta MBTs and is integrated with a combined day/night thermal imaging gunner's sight assembly with built-in laser rangefinder module and full meteorological parameter sensor package.

A full range of combat support vehicle models is being built to support the Arjun MBT fleet on the battlefield. These include an **ARRV**, an **AVLB** and a 155 mm self-propelled artillery chassis.

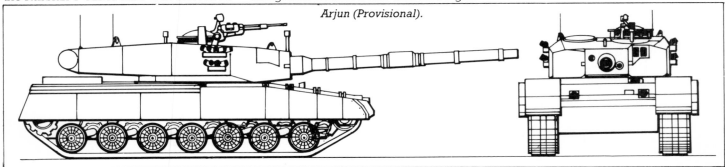

Arjun (Provisional).

Specification:
First prototype: ·1983-84
First production: 1993-current (initial batch of 126 to equip two regiments, at least 630 required for ten regiments with 500 plus due by year 2008-10)

Current user: India
Crew: 4
Combat weight: 58 000 kg
Max. road speed: 72 km/h
Powerpack: MTU MB 838 Ka 501 water-cooled diesel developing 1400 hp coupled

to a ZF automatic transmission
Armament: (main) 1 x 120 mm gun; (coaxial) 1 x 7.62 mm MG; (anti-aircraft) 1 x 7.62 mm MG; (smoke dischargers) x 6
No other reliable data is available.

Prototype of Arjun Mk 1 MBT.

Vijayanta

India

Under an agreement signed in 1961 India began the development with Vickers Defence Systems of its own indigenous tank production facility. The vehicle chosen for procurement was the **Vijayanta** (Indian name meaning Victorious) which was based on the Vickers Defence Systems Mk 1 MBT design. This was essentially a lighter version of the successful Centurion model with a stabilised 105 mm L7 series rifled main gun with the engine, transmission, fire control system and running gear of the early Chieftain models.

The first 90 vehicles were built in the UK and delivered to the Indian Army in 1967 to equip two Armoured Regiments: the 2nd Lancers and the 65th Armoured Regiment. The remainder of the 1400 odd vehicles were built over the period 1965-1983 at the Avadi Heavy Vehicles plant in India. The first Indian built Viyajantas were issued to the 67th Armoured Regiment.

By the December 1971 War with Pakistan the Indian army had six regiments of Vijayantas available: The 65th Armoured Regiment, 67th Armoured Regiment, 68th Armoured Regiment and 2nd Lancers all with the 1st Armoured Brigade, 1st Armoured Division as part of the uncommitted Indian Army HQ reserve – the division being rounded out by the 43 Lorried Infantry Brigade with 1 Sikh, 1 Jat and 1 Garwhal (Mechanised) Infantry Battalions equipped with OT-62 Topas tracked APCs, the divisional artillery with British Abbot 105 mm self-propelled guns and the 93rd Independent Armoured Reconnaissance Squadron with AMX-13s to provide close and medium reconnaissance; the 66 Armoured Regiment (as divisional armour for the 15th Infantry Division); and the 8th Light Cavalry (as part of the 3rd Armoured Brigade with the T-55 equipped Central India House and 72nd Armoured Regiments, and the 7th Grenadiers (Mechanised) Infantry Battalion using BTR-60 wheeled APCs).

In 1981 the Indian Army began its Project Bison upgrade programme for the Vijayanta. A total of 400 are being modernised with a license built MTU power pack utilizing the 750 hp MTU Series 837 V-8 Model MB833 Ka501 diesel engine, a Marconi Radar and Control Systems Limited fire control

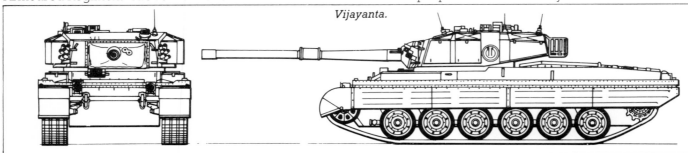

Vijayanta.

Specification:

First prototype: ·1963
First production: 1964-1983 (over 2200 built)
Current user: India
Crew: 4
Combat weight: 40 000 kg
Ground pressure: 0.89 kg/cm²
Length gun forwards: 9.8 m

Width (over skirts): 3.17 m
Height (without AA gun): 2.44 m
Max. road speed: 48 km/h
Maximum road range: 350-400 km
Fording: unprepared 1.14 m
Gradient: 60%
Side slope: 30%
Vertical obstacle: 0.91 m
Trench: 2.44 m

Powerpack: Leyland multi-fuel L60 diesel developing 650 hp and coupled to an SCG SN12 semi-automatic transmission
Armament: (main) 1 x 105 mm gun (44 rounds); (ranging) 1 x 12.7 mm MG (being replaced by modern fire control systems); (coaxial) 1 x 7.62 mm MG; (anti-aircraft) 1 x 7.62 mm MG; (smoke dischargers) 2 x 6

Indian Army Vijayanta MBT.

Vijayanta – continued

system, locally developed Jackal armour skirts, locally-developed Kanchan composite applique armour, the Hindustan Aeronautics GLN-2 gyro-based land navigation system, a semi-automatic loading system, an NBC protection system, a driver's night vision periscope, and new APFSDS-T ammunition. The 105 mm gun also uses locally designed and built APDS-T, HESH and smoke rounds.

A further 850 Vijayantas are being retrofitted with the locally designed computerised Bharat Electronics Tank Fire Control System Mk 1B (AL-4421) with Muzzle Reference System, improved gun laying facilities and laser rangefinder. Currently more than 25 Armoured Regiments use the Vijayanta.

A lengthened Vijayanta chassis has been produced for use with the 130 mm M-46 gun. The 100 or so self-propelled guns are known as the **HT-130 Catapult** and were followed by an **AVLB** version fitted with a 20 x 4 metre wide scissors bridge. Known as the **Kartik** this has been produced to supplement the existing Indian Army MT-55 bridgelayer tanks.

Other Vijayanta variants produced include an **ARV** version for use with the Vijayanta Armoured Regiments and a bulldozer version for preparing fire positions and crossing anti-tank obstacles.

A further 450 Vijayanta are likely to be converted to 155 mm self-propelled howitzers. This will include the fitting of the Vickers Shipbuilding & Engineering Ltd (VSEL) AS-90 turret onto the chassis but with a local 155 mm 39 calibre derivative of the Bofors FH-77B and 40 ready-use rounds.

Considerable modifications will be also made to the stretched chassis itself so that it can incorporate the 780 hp water-cooled diesel of the T-72 MBT, a Russian designed gearbox transmission and a locally built torsion bar suspension system. The first conversion is due to be off the Avadi conversion line in 1994. A tracked ammunition carrier to support the howitzer is also under development.

Vijayanta was replaced on the Avadi production line by a license built version of the Russian T-72M1 MBT know as the Ajeya, the first being delivered in 1988. By mid 1993, and including the original 500 direct delivery T-72G/T-72M1 (of which the first arrived in mid-1979 and were delivered to the 7th Cavalry Regiment in October of that year), a total of over 1400 were in service. These vehicles were due to undergo a major upgrade with the fitting of the Yugoslavian Rudi Cajavec integrated SUV-T72 digital Tank Fire Control System, a new weapons stabilisation system, new commander's day/night periscope and Kalchan applique armour. However, the Yugoslavian troubles have delayed the local production of the fire control system.

Opposite: Prototype VFM5 with 105mm main gun traversed to right.

VFM 5 Vickers Defence Systems/FMC   International

The **VFM 5** battle tank started life as a joint-venture project in 1985 between Vickers Defence Systems and FMC to produce a survivable light C-130H Hercules/C-141A/B, Starlifter/C-5A/B, Galaxy/C-17, Globemaster III air-portable/air droppable vehicle with the firepower capability to defeat most enemy tanks and armoured vehicles using APFSDS rounds and other battlefield targets using HESH rounds. To-date no order for the VFM 5 has been received.

The welded aluminium hull with add-on steel plates in the front and sides is almost identical to that used in the sophisticated FMC Close-Combat Vehicle – Light (CCV-L) produced as a private venture in the early eighties.

The turret is also of aluminium armour with add-on steel plate all round. The main armament is a Royal Ordnance 105 mm Low Recoil Force rifle gun with rigid thermal sleeve which fires APDS, APFSDS, HESH, smoke and canister round types. Alternative 105 mm calibre weapons can be mounted including a Rheinmetall super low recoil gun or a modified American M68 gun.

The gunner uses a Marconi Command and Control Systems computerised integrated fire control and electro-mechanical two-axis weapon stabilisation system with linked NANO-QUEST telescopic sight assembly. The latter has an integral laser rangefinder and Muzzle Reference System. A full set of back-up manual controls are fitted for use if the primary weapon controls fail.

The vehicle commander has his own Pilkington Optronics Raven combined day/night sight system but both he and the gunner can also have individual screen monitors linked to an optional thermal imaging unit for night fighting.

The powerpack is fitted at the vehicle rear with access being provided by a rear hull ramp. All the fitter has to do once the ramp is lowered is to slide the unit out on its rails and perform the necessary maintenance checks/repairs.

No combat support vehicles have been designed on the VFM 5 chassis.

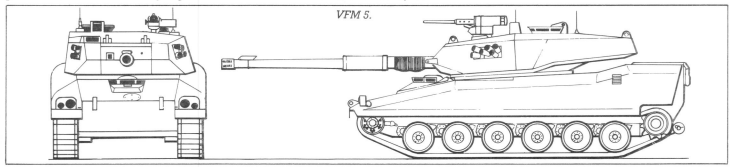

VFM 5.

Specification:

First prototype: ·1986
First production: none, ready for production on receipt of an order
Crew: 4
Combat weight: 19 750 kg
Ground pressure: 0.69 kg/cm²
Length gun forwards: 8.61 m
Width: 2.69 m
Height (without AA gun): 2.35 m
Ground clearance: 0.41 m
Fording: unprepared 1.3 m
Gradient: 60%
Side slope: 40%
Vertical obstacle: 0.8 m
Trench: 2.1 m
Powerpack: Detroit Diesel 6V-92TA diesel developing 550 hp coupled to an HMPT-500-3 automatic transmission
Armament: (main) 1 x 105 mm gun (41 rounds); (coaxial) 1 x 7.62 mm MG; (anti-aircraft) 1 x 7.62 mm or 12.7 mm MG; (smoke dischargers) 2 x 6

Prototype of VFM 5 at speed.

T-55 variants

As a result of the Gulf War with Iran the Iraqi Army requested its Ministry of Defence to develop a local armoured vehicle manufacturing/modernisation industrial capability.

Three of the programmes which resulted from this approach involved what could be done with the many thousands of Soviet T-54/55 and Chinese Type 59/69 series MBTs that were in use with the Iraqi Army.

These are:

Multilayer armour T-55/Type 69 – this involves the fitting of add-on multilayer special composite armour packages to the upper glacis area, hull front and turret front and sides, a hinged stand-off armoured screen at the turret front and sides, a hinged stand-off armoured screen at the turret

rear to act as a counterbalance to the weight of the armour added at the turret front and modern night vision equipment. With these modifications the combatweight of the modified carrier tank is increased by approximately 4600 kg. Only a few tanks were seen with this modification and all seemed to be associated with the Iraqi 5th Mechanised Division used in the battles around Khafji. The tanks, mostly modified T-55s, were apparently assigned to tank company commanders.

Modernised T-54 – it is believed that Iraq had modernised a small number of its old T-54 MBTs using elements of the Romanian T-55 upgrade kit (qv).

Rebuilt T-55 – in what is probably the most capable of the armoured vehicle

modernisation programmes undertaken by Iraq a small number of T-55 MBTs have been totally rebuilt with a raised turret accommodating a locally built Soviet 125 mm 2A46 D81T smoothbore gun complete with its autoloader system, new armoured side skirts, re-arranged turret stowage facilities, four-round electrically-fired smoke discharge assemblies and new passive night vision equipment for the crew.

The fire control system has also been upgraded to a computerised system standard using component elements for the fire control system model used in the Soviet T-72 MBT.

It is probable that several countries have helped Iraq with this particular modification programme including

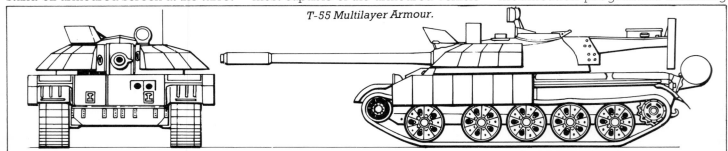

T-55 Multilayer Armour.

Egypt, Romania and Yugoslavia. Iraq has also modified numbers of its T-62 series medium tanks and has a T-series rebuild facility for its Chinese and Russian T-54/55/Type 59/Type 69 family of medium tanks. Licensed production from former eastern bloc countries of the T-72 MBT is also undertaken on a small scale under the name Babylon Lion (Assad Bablye).

Specification:
First prototype: ·mid eighties
First production: mid eighties
Current user: Iraq
Crew: Multilayer Armour T-55/Type 69 – 4; Rebuilt T-55 – 3
Armament: (main) Multilayer Armour T-55/Type 69 1 x 100 mm gun, rebuilt T-55 1 x 125 mm gun; (coaxial) 1 x 7.62 mm MG; (bow) 1 x 7.62 mm MG; (anti-aircraft) 1 x 7.62 mm MG; (smoke dischargers) 2 x 4

No other reliable information is available.

Captured Iraqi Army T-55 Multilayer Armour variant Second Gulf War.

Merkava Mk 3/Mk 4 Israel

Externally the **Merkava Mk 3** appears very similar to the two earlier Merkava marks apart from the main gun, which is a 120 mm Israeli designed and built smoothbore cannon with a distinctive Vishay Israel thermal sleeve. However, practically every major component is in fact new.

The armour package is of an advanced special passive type that is integrated into the basic tank design and contains approximately 50% of its make-up as replaceable modules. The latter allows for both easier deport level repairs and replacement by more modern armour developments as they become available.

The basic cast steel turret has attachments for special armour modules at the front and sides, as have the hull glacis, sponsons and nose positions. Full length special armour side skirts are also provided. All-electric turret/weapon drive and stabilisation systems are fitted to reduce the internal fire risk.

An advanced director/hunter-killer type computerised fire control system with retractable meteorological sensor has been fitted. This significantly increases the first-round kill probability against moving targets. An Amcoram 360 degree capability warning system is used to provide warning of enemy lasing and electromagnetic emissions.

The main gun fires both Israeli and standard NATO type 120 mm smoothbore ammunition families. Like the Mk 1/2 the two 7.62 mm FN MAG anti-aircraft machine guns carried are a specially modified version developed for the **Merkava** family with variable height capability mounts. The 12.7 mm MG is mounted over the main gun and again is electrically fired from within the turret. Six-round launchers for the CL-3030 IS-6 smoke screen system grenades are fitted wither side of the turret front. A new central Filter and over pressurisation system is carried for NBC defence.

Similar command and combat engineer models to the Merkava Mk 1/2 are also used. Further improvements are being made to the vehicle including the fitting of an upgraded

Merkava Mk 3.

final drive assembly to cope with the additional weight. Vehicles modified in this manner are being referred to as the **Merkava Mk 4**. A further version with a 140 mm main gun is likely.

Specification:

First prototype: ·Merkava Mk 3 1986; Merkava Mk 4 1989/90

First production: Mk 3 1987-current (approx 350 built to-date); Mk 4 1992-current (modifications of built vehicles)

Current user: Israel

Crew: 4
Combat weight: 62 000 kg
Ground pressure: 0.96 kg/cm^2
Length gun forwards: 8.78 m
Width (with skirts): 3.7 m
Height (without AA gun): 2.76 m
Ground clearance: 0.53 m
Max. road speed: 55 km/h
Maximum range: 500 km
Fording: unprepared 1.4 m
Gradient: 70%
Side slope: 40%
Vertical obstacle: 1 m

Trench: 3.5 m
Powerpack: TCM AVDS-1790-9AR air cooled turbo-charged diesel developing 1200 hp coupled to an Ashot fully automatic transmission
Armament: (main) 1 x 120 mm gun (50 rounds); (coaxial) 1 x 7.62 mm MG; (anti-aircraft) 1 x 12.7 mm and 2 x7.62 mm MG; (anti-personnel) 1 x 60 mm light mortar (internally loaded); (smoke dischargers) 2 x 6

Israeli Army Merkava Mk 3 MBT.

Merkava Mk 1/Mk 2   Israel

The **Merkava (Chariot)** MBT design is the brainchild of the legendary Israeli Armoured Corps officer Major General Israel Tal and is based on the concept that the survivability of the tank crew is the prime factor rather than the more usual trade-off areas of armour protection, firepower and mobility. Using this starting point General Tal and his design team made every part of the Merkava play its part in providing protection for the crew. The engine was placed at the front of the tank, the most suitable ballistic armour shapes and structures were found for the low profile turret and hull and the protected fuel tanks, ammunition bins and equipment

stowage areas were used to provide 'spaced armour' type protection around the crew compartment. The commander's position even has a special collapsible umbrella type top protection armour device to allow for the classic Israeli 'open hatch' combat operation. A rear two-piece crew escape/ammunition loading hatch/troop embarkation-disembarkation system is also fitted.

This crew safety concept was validated in the 1982 Peace for Galilee War as only 7 Merkava Mk 1 tanks were totally destroyed (compared to 8 Sho't and 37 Mag'ach) in Lebanon. None of the Merkava losses resulted from secondary ammunition explosions due

to enemy fire and, more importantly, no Merkava had any of its crewmen killed.

In combat against the Syrian tanks the Merkava destroyed a large number of Soviet supplied T-55 and T-62 medium tanks as well as several T-72 vehicles. It also proved to be quite a useful vehicle for fighting in built-up areas by providing both a mobile firepower base and a means to safely transport troops.

The main armament is the Israeli made 105 mm M68 rifled gun firing HEAT, HESH, canister and APFSDS-T ammunition. A Matador Mk 1 computerised fire control system is fitted.

The **Merkava Mk 2** introduced addi-

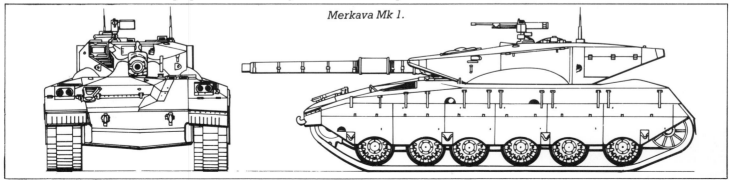

Merkava Mk 1.

tional special passive armour protection on the turret front and sides and hull front, new special armour side skirts and powerpack transmission system, a MK2 Matador FCS and an hanging chain steel ball protection system for the turret rear.

Both Merkava marks have command tank variants with additional radios and can be fitted with the Track Width Mine Plough (TWMP) and the RKM mine-clearing roller system for the combat engineer role. All MK 1 and Mk 2 vehicles are being brought up to near the **Merkava Mk 3** production standard with the fitting of selected components as they undergo deep base maintenance. However, they retain their 105 mm main armament.

It is interesting to note that large numbers of Merkava (all marks) are given individual names. All crewmen also carry their own small arms for self defence and have a wide range of squad defence weapons available.

The only known variant of the Merkava is the **155 mm Slammer self-propelled artillery vehicle** using a locally designed and built turret (mounting a 155 mm Soltam gun-howitzer) and a modified Merkava chassis. As far as it is known the Israeli Army has not yet placed any order for the Slammer.

Specification:
First prototype: ·Mk 1 1974; Mk 2 1982
First production: Mk 1 1979-83 (approx 330 built); Mk 2 1983-90 (approx 600 built)
Current user: Israel
Crew: 4 (plus infantry/sapper squad)
Combat weight: 63 000 kg
Ground pressure: 0.9 kg/cm²
Length gun forwards: 8.63 m
Width (with skirts): 3.7 m
Height (without AA gun): 2.75 m
Ground clearance: 0.47 m
Max. road speed: 46 km/h
Maximum range: Mk 1 400 km; Mk 2 500 km
Fording: unprepared 1.4 m
Gradient: 60%

Side slope: 40%
Vertical obstacle: 0.95 m
Trench: 3 m
Powerpack: Mk 1 – TCM AVDS-1790-6A V-12 air-cooled turbo-charged diesel developing 908 hp and coupled to an Allison CD-850-6B powershift crossdrive transmission; Mk 2 – same diesel engine but with an Ashot transmission
Armament: (main) 1 x 105 mm gun (62 rounds); (coaxial) 1 x 7.62 mm MG; (anti-aircraft) 1 x 12.7 mm and 2 x 7.62 mm MG; (anti-personnel) 1 x 60 mm light mortar (Mk 1 external, Mk 2 internal)

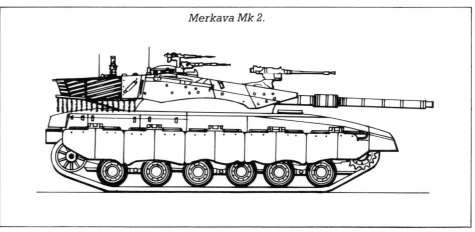

Merkava Mk 2.

Merkava Mk 2 MBT of the Israeli Army.

Mag'ach (Upgraded M48/M60 series Patton)   Israel

M48 Modified Patton – the original 200 ex-West German M48A2C procured in 1962-4 and modified during 1966-68 with 105 mm L7 rifled main gun and minor stowage arrangements. Approximately 40 served in the 1967 Six Day War, the remaining M48 Pattons used by the Israelis were the 90 mm gun version.

M48 Upgraded Patton (or Mag'ach) – Some 600 plus Modified M48, M48, M48A1, M48A2 and M48A3 model vehicles upgraded 1968-75 (and unofficially called M48A4 by the Americans) to an equivalent M60 standard with V-12 AV-1790-2A diesel engine, new transmission, modified air filter boxes, low profile commander's cupola and VSS-2 white light/infra-red searchlight. Used extensively in 1973 Yom Kippur War.

M48 Mag'ach (Blazer ERA) – 1979-80 conversions of the Improved M48 Mag'ach together with over 150 M48A5 procured 1997-79 for Blazer reactive armour and heavier anti-aircraft/personnel armament. Used extensively in 1982 Lebanon War.

M60/M60A1 Mag'ach – standard models procured 1970-77 and modified with Israeli equipment such as radios, stowage facilities etc. M60A1 version used in 1973 Yom Kippur war.

M60/M60A1 Mag'ach (M1980) – the original M60 series Mag'ach tanks further upgraded with Blazer reactive armour, a new Israeli fire control system, CL-3030 IS-10 smoke discharger system, and heavier anti-aircraft/personnel armament. Used extensively in 1982 Lebanon War.

Mag'ach 7 – standard M60A3 model procured from 1979 onwards and rebuilt 1988 onwards with new passive armour package for turret, hull and side skirts, new diesel engine, transmission and tracks and new state-of-the art fire control system equivalent to that fitted to the Merkava Mk 3. The designation 7 may well mean that there have been six previous Mag'ach

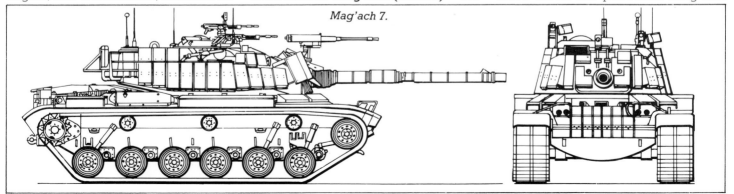

Mag'ach 7.

Mag'ach – continued

model standards.

Support vehicles based on the Mag'ach chassis include the standard Israeli Army MBT bulldozer blade, Full Track Width Mineplough and Mine Roller conversions by using add-on kits.

The 17 **M88** and 30 **M88A1 ARV** used by the Israeli Army and based on M48 automative components Army have also been upgraded with the Blazer reactive armour and heavier anti-aircraft/personnel weapon package.

The Israelis also operate some 50 odd **M48/M60 AVLBs** and 15 **M728 Combat Engineer Vehicles** all with local modifications.

Specification:

First prototype: ·1966
First production: 1967-current (progressive upgrade programmes –some 800 M48 series and 1400 M60 series Pattons converted)
Current user: Israel (400 plus M48 and 1400 M60 Mag'achs)
Crew: 4
Combat weight: M48 Mag'ach and 0M6/0A1 Mag'ach include 1000 kg of Blazer ERA blocks

Powerpack: M48/M60/M60A1 Mag'ach TCM AV1790-2A V-12 air-cooled diesel developing 750 hp and coupled to an Allison CD-850-6 automatic transmission; M60A3 Mag'ach TCM AVDS1790-6A V-12 air-cooled diesel engine developing 908 hp and coupled to an Allison CD-850-6B automatic transmission
Armament: (main) 1 x 105 mm gun; (coaxial) 1 x 7.62 mm MG; (anti-aircraft) 1 x 12.7 mm and 2 x7.62 mm MG; (anti-personnel) 1 x 60 mm light mortar
No other accurate information is available.

Israeli Army Ma'gach with Blazer reactive armour package.

Sho't (Upgraded Centurion) Israel

The Centurion Mk 3 entered operational service with the Israeli Ground Defence Force in 1960. Training and combat experience soon showed that the vehicle needed upgrading from the 20 pdr armament and petrol engine state so the Israeli Ordnance Corps undertook its first Centurion modification programme of the Mk 3 and Mk 5 in 1963. This involved the replacement of the gun by the 105 mm M68/L7 series rifled gun and an increase in basic ammunition load from 70 to 72 rounds. the 105 mm can fire locally produced HEAT, APFSDS-T, HESH and canister rounds and easily penetrates T-54/55/62 MBT frontal armour at 1800 metres range.

In 1967 trials were conducted to establish a new engine type for the Cent-urion which was safer to operate in combat conditions, provided better range, improved engine cooling and air filtration. The engine ultimately selected was the air-cooled AVDS-1790-2A, the same as being used in the M48 Patton fleet.

The first Upgrade Centurions, known by the Israeli name **Sho't (Whip)** entered service in 1970 and were characterised by their elevated engine deck and external box air filters.

Following the 1973 the Sho'ts were again refitted with additional modifications including a low profile commander's cupola, additional anti-personnel weapons, Blazer explosive reactive armour (ERA) boxes and a CL-3030 IS-10 smoke screen system. The latest Sho't configuration (with around 1000 in service) being that given in the specification table.

Other versions of the Sho't are:

Nagmasho't – 100 plus conversions from Sho't MBT to produce a heavy APC for use by the Combat Engineer Corps sappers. The turret is removed and replaced by an infantry compartment for eight sappers with raised sloping side armour grilles, new passive heavy armour side skirts and attachments for Blazer ERA blocks. The anti-personnel armament is three 7.62 mm FN MAG pintle mounted MGs and three 52 or 60 mm light mortars.

Support vehicles – **Sho't/ABK-3** and **Sho't/RKM** bulldozer tanks, **Sho't/TWMP** and **Sho't/RK** mine-clearing roller vehicles, **Sho't MRL** with four 290 mm calibre unguided rockets.

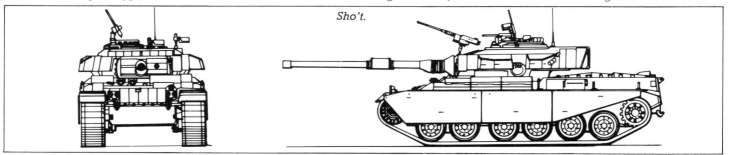

Sho't.

Sho't – continued

Specification:
First prototype: ·1967
First production: 1968-74 modernisation programme (approx 1400 converted)
Current user: Israel
Crew: 4
Combat weight: 51 800 kg (+ 1000 kg Blazer ERA)
Ground pressure: n/va
Length gun forwards: 9.83 m
Width (with skirts): 3.4 m
Height (without AA gun): 2.96 m
Ground clearance: 0.46 m
Max. road speed: 43.2 km/h
Maximum range: 400 km
Fording: unprepared 1.5 m
Gradient: 60%
Side slope: 40%
Vertical obstacle: 0.9 m
Trench: 3.4 m
Powerpack: TCM AVDS-1790-2A V-12 air cooled diesel developing 750 hp coupled to an Allison CD-850-6 automatic powershift crossdrive transmission
Armament: (main) 1 x 105 mm gun (72 rounds); (coaxial) 1 x 7.62 mm MG; (anti-aircraft) 1 x 12.7 mm and 2 x7.62 mm MG; (anti-personnel) 1 x 52 or 60 mm light mortar; (smoke dischargers) 2 x 10

Modified Centurion of Israeli Army before final rebuild to full Sh'ot standard.

M51 Isherman (M51 Sherman)   Israel

The **M51 Sherman** was conceived in the early sixties as a cost effective Israeli Armoured Corps answer to the Soviet T-54/T-55 tanks entering service with the Arab Armies.

Using the extensive knowledge gained during the remanufacturing of the earlier 50 M50 Mk 1 and 200 plus M50 Mk 2 Shermans the Israeli Ordnance Corps took approx 250 M4A1 type cast hulls and rebuilt them by adding a Cummins 460 hp diesel engine (with reworked engine space) and transmission, the wide track E8 Horizontal Volute Spring Suspension (HVSS) system and a completely rebuilt turret housing a specially manufactured GIAT 105 mm CN D1514 L44 800 m/s muzzle velocity shorter derivative of the standard French Army 105 mm CN 105F1 L56 rifled tank gun and a longer and heavier counterweight at the rear of the turret bustle.

The gun also had a distinctive muzzle brake (similar to but not the same as that fitted to the French AML-90 armoured car) and new gun control systems. The ammunition types used were locally designed and built HEAT, HE and smoke round versions of the original French ammunition.

The M51 was subsequently used by Reserve Armoured Brigades in both the 1967 June War and 1973 Yom Kippur Wars where its gun proved highly effective in penetrating all the front, turret and side armour plate of the Soviet T-54/55/62 tank models at standard 1000 metre battle ranges.

Although now long gone from front-line Israeli Army service it served its remaining years with several of the Territorial Command reserve tank companies specially trained for border region tank-infantry support operations. A number of surplus M51s were also sold to the Chilian Army, where they remain in service.

The **M50 Sherman Mk 2** armed with the French 75 mm CN75-50 tank gun and firing AP and HE rounds found use with the South Lebanese Army and the Lebanese Forces Militia. The tanks were given as military aid by the Israelis. The latest use of these vehicles was by the Lebanese Forces Militia in its 1990 battles north of Beirut with

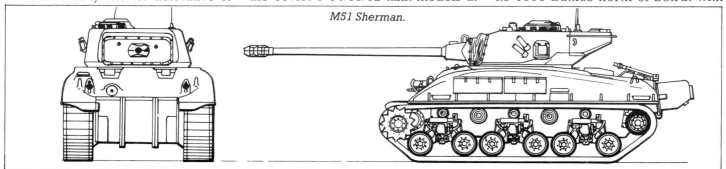

M51 Sherman.

General Aoun's Christian Army where they were seen fighting unsuccessful tank battles with M48A5 Pattons.

Other Israeli Army vehicles based on modifications of M4/M50 chassis include the Israeli Artillery's **155 mm L33 self-propelled gun-howitzer,** the **155 mm M50 self-propelled gun-howitzer**, the **36-round 240 mm Multiple Rocket Launcher**, the **4-round 290 mm Multiple Rocket Launcher** and the **160 mm Soltam self-propelled mortar vehicles**. There were also **armoured command post, armoured ambulance** (two types), **armoured artillery observation post** (only three built with a 30m high hydraulically operated observation post for use on the Suez Canal Front during the War of Attrition) and several types of armoured engineer vehicle conversions (the **Trail Blazer armoured engineer assault tank,** the **M4 Armoured Engineer Bulldozer tank** and the locally modified **M32 ARV** (with Cummins engine, HVSS wide track suspension and M50/51 standard oil, electrical and fuel systems).

Other **M4 Sherman** derivatives used include the **M74 ARV**, the **M4 'Crab' mine clearing tank** and a locally modified **Mobile Live Target Tank**. A number of the Egyptian modified **M4A2 Shermans** that were fitted with the turret and 75 mm gun of the AMX-13 light tank were also taken into service following capture in the 1967 War. However, they were subsequently modified in Israeli service to carry the 75 mm main gun from the M50 Sherman.

Specification:
First prototype: ·1960
First production: 1963-66 (?)
(250 plus built)

Current user: Chile
Crew: 4
Combat weight: 39 000 kg
Max. road speed: 46 km/h
Maximum range: 270 km
Powerpack: Cummins diesel developing 460 hp coupled to a manual transmission
Armament: (main) 1 x 105 mm gun; (coaxial) 1 x 7.62 mm MG; (anti-aircraft) 1 x 12.7 mm or 7.62 mm MG; (anti-personnel) 1 x 52 or 60 mm light mortar; (smoke dischargers) 2 x 4
No other accurate data is available.

Israeli Army M-51 Sherman during operations in Sinai desert.

OTO Melara/IVECO Fiat **C-1 Ariete**   Italy

The **C-1 Ariete (Ram)** MBT has been developed by OTO-Melara with the assistance of FIAT/IVECO to meet a 1982 Italian Army specification for a long term replacement for the obsolete M47 Patton tanks used by the Italian Army. An order for an initial production batch of 200 vehicles was placed in 1992 for delivery from 1993 onwards.

The vehicle uses special composite armour in the construction of its hull and turret giving the latter the typical slab sided appearance of modern MBTs. The main armament is an OTO-Melara designed and built 120 mm L44 smoothbore gun with thermal sleeve, fume extractor and Muzzle Reference System firing Italian made NATO standard equivalent APFSDS-T and HEAT-MP-T smoothbore ammunition.

The fire control system is the latest generation computerised full solution modular Officine Galileo TURMS model which, together with gunner's and commander's optical day/thermal vision night sight assemblies and laser rangefinder module, allows high single shot kill probability engagements against both moving and stationary. targets whilst the Ariete itself is either moving or stationary. If the primary fire control system fails completely then the gunner can use a manual back-up periscopic sight with a set of aiming graticules.

To complete the night fighting capabilities of the vehicle the driver has facilities for a passive night driving periscope to be fitted.

Although none have been noted yet it is highly probable that support vehicle versions of the Ariete will be developed over the next few years. These are expected to include **ARRV** and **AVLB** variants so as to simplify logistic problems within the Ariete equipped armoured units by equipping them with a single armoured vehicle chassis type and its ancillary systems such as powerpacks and suspensions.

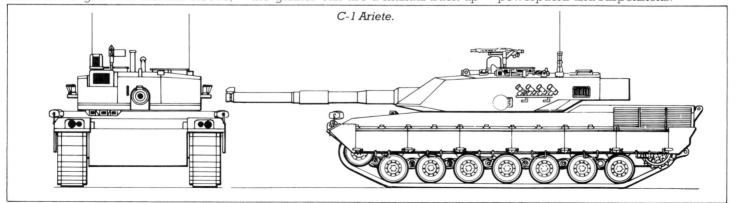

C-1 Ariete.

Specification:

First prototype: 1986
First production: 1993-current (initial order for 200)
Current user: Italy
Crew: 4
Combat weight: 54 000 kg
Ground pressure: 0.85 kg/cm²
Length gun forwards: 9.67 m
Width (with skirts): 3.6 m

Height (without AA gun): 2.5 m
Ground clearance: 0.44 m
Max. road speed: 66 km/h
Maximum range: 550-600 km
Fording: unprepared 1.2 m
Gradient: 60%
Side slope: 30%
Vertical obstacle: 2.1 m
Trench: 3 m
Powerpack: IVECO FIAT MTCA V-12

turbocharged diesel developing 1250 hp coupled to a ZF LSG 3000 automatic transmission
Armament: (main) 1 x 120 mm gun (42 rounds); (coaxial) 1 x 7.62 mm MG; (anti-aircraft) 1 x 7.62 mm MG; (smoke dischargers) 2 x 4

C1-Ariete MBT during cross-country trials.

OTO Melara **OF-40 Mk 1/Mk 2**   **Italy**

Between 1974 and 1983 OTO Melara built 720 Leopard 1 MBT under licence from Germany and prior to this the Italian Army took delivery of 200 vehicles direct from Krauss-Maffei. For a number of reasons OTO Melara could not export the Leopard 1 MBT so developed the **OF-40** MBT specifically for the export market, although it did incorporate certain features of the late production Leopard 1A4 which was not built in Italy. In the designation O stands for OTO Melara, F for FIAT who were responsible for the automotive components and 40 for the original design weight in tonnes. By early 1990 there had been only one customer for the OF-40, the UAE, which took delivery of 18 Mk 1 vehicles followed by a second batch of 18 Mk 2 vehicles, the

original Mk 1s being subsequently upgraded to the later mark standard. Production can be restarted if additional orders are received by OTO Melara.

The OF-40 is of conventional MBT design with driver's compartment at front, turret in centre and powerpack at rear with the hull and turret being of all welded steel construction. Main armament comprises a 105 mm rifled gun designed by OTO Melara which can fire standard NATO ammunition including APFSDS, a 7.62 mm machine gun is mounted coaxial with the main armament and a 12.7 mm or 7.62 mm machine gun is mounted on the roof for local anti-personnel and air defence purpose.

The original **OF-40 Mk 1** MBT had a

simple fire but the **MK 2** has a computerised fire control system that includes a ballistic computer, various sensors, gunner's sight incorporating a laser rangefinder, stabilisation system for 105 mm gun, roof mounted stabilised sight for the tank commander and LLLTV camera over the gun mantlet.

Standard equipment on the OF-40 includes a deep fording system, an overpressure NBC system and, for the driver, a night system.

A batch of three **ARVs** based on the OF-40 MBT chassis was built for the UAE. The ARV has a crew of four and weighs some 45 000 kg in combat configuration.

A modified OF-40 chassis has been used for the prototype **OTO Melara**

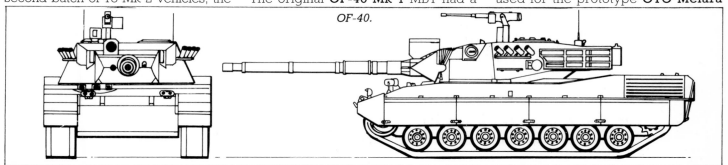

OF-40.

OF-40 Mk 2 MBT of UAE (Abu Dhabi) Army.

OTOMATIC 76 mm anti-aircraft turret and the **OTO Melara 155 mm Palmeria self-propelled howitzer.** The Palmeria has been sold to Libya, Nigeria and one other country. The Palmeria turret has also been sold to Argentina for use on a modified TAM chassis.

Specification:

First prototype: 1980
First production: 1981-1985 (36 built to-date)

Current user: UAE
Crew: 4
Combat weight: 45 500 kg
Ground pressure: 0.92 kg/cm²
Length gun forwards: 9.2 m
Width (with skirts): 3.5 m
Height (without AA gun): 2.68 m
Ground clearance: 0.44 m
Max. road speed: 60 km/h
Maximum range: 600 km
Fording: 1.2 m
Gradient: 60%

Side slope: 30%
Vertical obstacle: 1.1 m
Trench: 3 m
Powerpack: MTU MB 838 Ca M-500 V-10 diesel developing 830 hp coupled to a ZF automatic transmission
Armament: (main) 1 x 105 mm gun (57 rounds); (coaxial) 1 x 7.62 mm MG; (anti-aircraft) 1 x 12.7 mm MG; (smoke dischargers) 2 x 4

ARV based on OF-40 MBT chassis, one of three built for the UAE (Abu Dhabi) Army.

Mitsubishi **Type 90**   # **Japan**

The **Mitsubishi Type 90** MBT is the long-term Japanese Ground Self-Defence Force third generation MBT replacement for its elderly first generation Type 61 MBTs. Like most of the Japanese military programmes the Type 90 development period has been protracted and when eventually produced at the typically Japanese slow yearly production rate will be the most expensive unit cost MBT produced to-date by any nation.

The tank hull and turret feature special composite armour in their construction with the latter having the characteristic slab sided appearance of modern western MBTs. The crew has been cut to three by the adoption of an automatic loading system for the license built 120 mm Rheinmetall smoothbore tank gun which gives APFSDS-T and HEAT-MP-T rounds. The tank suspension is of a hybrid torsion/hydropneumatic type allowing it to tilt forwards or backwards for gun aiming in difficult terrain and together with the running gear is protected by armoured side skirts.

The fire control system is of the latest full solution digital computerised hunter-killer/director type with integral gunner and commander's sight thermal imaging day/night capabilities. The gunner also has a laser range-finder module attached to his sight.

The driver is provided with a full night driving facility and an NBC system is a standard feature. No export sales are envisaged during the production period of the vehicle.

Although only the **Type 90 ARV combat support vehicle** has been produced to-date it is likely that **AVLB** and **AEV** models are being designed to eventually replace Type 61 derivatives.

Right: The Type 90 MBT, probably the most expensive tank in the world as the production rate is so slow.

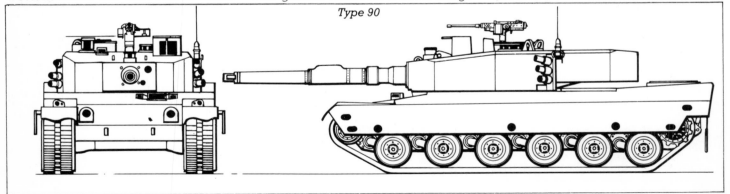

Type 90

Specification:

First prototype: 1982
First production: 1992-current (132 ordered against total vehicle requirement of 400-500)
Current user: Japan
Crew: 3
Combat weight: 50 000 kg
Ground pressure: 0.89 kg/cm²
Length gun forwards: 9.76 m
Width (with skirts): 3.43 m
Height (without AA gun): 2.34 m
Ground clearance: 0.45 m normal; 0.2-0.6 m variable
Max. road speed: 70 km/h
Maximum range: about 350 km
Fording: unprepared 2 m
Gradient: 60%
Side slope: 40%
Vertical obstacle: 1 m
Trench: 2.7 m
Powerpack: Mitsubishi 10ZG V-10 fuel injection diesel developing 1500 hp coupled to an automatic transmission
Armament: (main) 1 x 120 mm gun (40 rounds); (coaxial) 1 x 7.62 mm MG; (anti-aircraft) 1 x 12.7 mm MG; (smoke dischargers) 2 x 3

The Type 90 MBT, probably the most expensive tank in the world as the production rate is so slow.

Mitsubishi **Type 74**   **Japan**

The **Mitsubishi Type 74** second generation MBT took 11 years to develop from the conception stage to the pre-production series prototype configuration. It has subsequently been produced over a 16 year period from 1975 onwards at the ridiculously low average yearly rate of 50 odd vehicles. A fact which has made the Type 74 an inordinately expensive MBT in terms of unit cost.

It has, however, due to its cross-linked hydro-pneumatic suspension system – a very unusual aspect – the capability to raise or lower itself completely, to tilt itself either forwards or backwards and to incline itself to either side – so as to match its ground clearance to the terrain it is moving over or to enable it to engage targets either high or lower than the main guns normal elevation/depression limits can accommodate.

The gun itself is a locally built Royal Ordnance 105 mm L7 series rifled tank gun firing APFSDS-T, HESH-T, APDS-T and smoke type ammunition. A basic computerised ballistic fire control system is used with inputs from a laser rangefinder module at the commander's sight assembly.

The crew has an NBC system whilst a white light/infra-red searchlight is fitted to the left of the main gun for night fighting. The driver has a set of active infra-red night driving lights.

A support variant of the basic Type 74 MBT has been produced by fitting a bulldozer blade kit to the vehicle front. In addition small lnumbers of the **Type 78 ARV** have been built using the Type 74 chassis.

The last combat variant is, however, the **Type 87** twin 35 mm self-propelled anti-aircraft gun tank. Approximately 200 are to be produced in the nineties on a modified Type 74 chassis to replace the current fifties vintage American twin 40 mm M42 vehicles.

The Type 87 has independent all-weather search and tracking radars mounted on the rear of the turret which has the 35 mm automatic cannon mounted externally on either side in a Gepard-style arrangement.

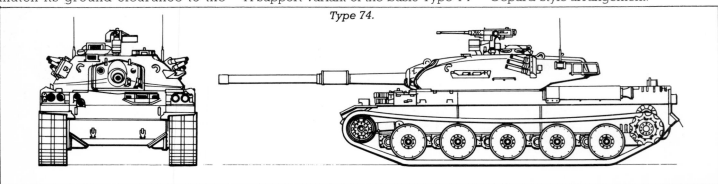

Type 74.

Specification:
First prototype: 1969
First production: 1975-1991 (873 built)
Current user: Japan
Crew: 4
Combat weight: 38 000 kg
Ground pressure: 0.86 kg/cm^2
Length gun forwards: 9.42 m
Width: 3.2 m
Height (without AA gun): 2.48 m
Ground clearance: 0.2-0.65 m variable
Max. road speed: 55 km/h
Maximum range: 300 km
Fording: unprepared 1 m
Gradient: 60%
Side slope: 40%
Vertical obstacle: 1 m
Trench: 2.7 m
Powerpack: Mitsubishi 10ZF V-10 liquid-cooled diesel developing 720 hp coupled to a Mitsubishi MT75A manual transmission
Armament: (main) 1 x 105 mm gun (55 rounds); (coaxial) 1 x 7.62 mm MG; (anti-aircraft) 1 x 12.7 mm MG; (smoke dischargers) 2 x 3

Type 74, the standard MBT of the Japanese Ground Self-Defence Force.

Mitsubishi Type 61   Japan

The **Mitsubishi Type 61** was the first indigenous Japanese designed and developed post-war MBT and can be considered a first generation equivalent of the American M47 Patton but built specifically for the oriental stature. The Type 61 was used mainly as an infantry support tank assigned to the tank battalion attached to each Infantry Division. These units each have four tank companies which comprise three four vehicle MBT platoons and a small armoured reconnaissance detachment (with two reconnaissance vehicles). The Type 61 is also used as a training vehicle at the various armour and infantry schools.

Retirement of the vehicle started in late 1984 with a progressive replacement programme underway as initially the Type 74 were delivered followed by the Type-61 replacement new-build Type 90 MBTs are delivered.

The installed main gun is the 90 mm Type 61 rifled tank gun with fume extractor and muzzle brake. The gunner uses a basic coincidence type optical rangefinder sight.

No NBC system is fitted although almost all remaining vehicles have been retrofitted with active infra-red driving lights and a white light/infra-red searchlight to the left of the main gun to provide a limited night fighting capability.

The Type 61 chassis has also been used as the basis for a number of combat support vehicles; the **Type 67 AVLB** with scissors bridge; the **Type 67 AEV** fitted with a light crane and bulldozer blade for battlefield combat engineer use; and the **Type 70 ARV** conversion whereby the turret of the basic tank has been removed and replaced by a open sided super-structure mounting a winch and an 'A'-frame for heavy component lifting on the battlefield.

It is expected that by the end of the current decade all the Type 61 MBT variants will have been scrapped.

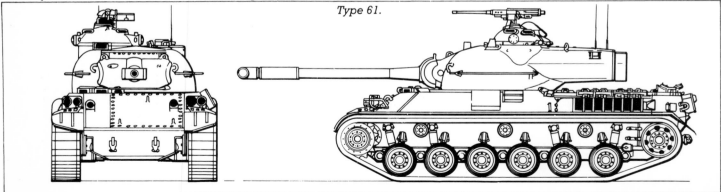

Type 61.

Specification:

First prototype: 1957
First production: 1962-1973 (559 built)
Current user: Japan
Crew: 4
Combat weight: 35 000 kg
Ground pressure: 0.95 kg/cm²
Length gun forwards: 8.2 m
Width: 2.95 m
Height (without AA gun): 2.5 m
Ground clearance: 0.4 m
Max. road speed: 45 km/h
Maximum range: 200 km
Fording: unprepared 1 m
Gradient: 60%
Side slope: 30%
Vertical obstacle: 0.7 m
Trench: 2.5 m
Powerpack: Mitsubishi 12-HM21WT V-12 turbocharged diesel developing 600 hp coupled to a manual transmission
Armament: (main) 1 x 90 mm gun (65 rounds); (coaxial) 1 x 7.62 mm MG; (anti-aircraft) 1 x 12.7 mm MG; (smoke dischargers) 2 x 3

Top right: Type 61 MBT of Japanese Ground Self-Defence Force.
Below: Type 70 ARV variant of Type 61 MBT.

Vickers Defence Systems Khalid   Jordan

The **Khalid** MBT programme resulted from the defunct Shah of Iran's order for FV4030/2 Shir 1 and FV4030/3 Shir 2 MBTs that was cancelled in 1979 by the Islamic Iranian government. Jordan then ordered 274 Khalid tanks that are essentially similar to the Shir 1 model but with minor changes in equipment to suit Jordanian Army requirements.

The FV4030/2 was based on the Chieftain Mk 5 design but with evolutionary changes to overcome problems encountered in service. These included a new 1200 hp engine, a new automatic transmission and the fitting of an improved bogie type suspension. The main armament is a Royal Ordnance 120 mm L11A5 rifled gun with fume extractor, thermal sleeve and Muzzle Reference System. Ammunition types used include smoke, HESH, APDS and/or APFSDS. These are loaded into the breech with either a separate bag or rigid combustible case charge. The turret mounted 7.62 mm MG can be fired from inside the commander's station.

The fire control system is the Computer Sighting System derivative of the British Army's Chieftain IFCS and is used with the gunner's Barr & Stroud Tank Laser Sight unit. Full NBC equipment, a Pilkington Optronics Condor passive day/night sight assembly at the commander's station and a Pilkington Optronics Passive Night Vision periscope for the driver (in lieu of his day driving periscope) are also fitted.

Although no support vehicle variants of the **Khalid** have been developed it is known that Jordan has purchased approximately 30 undelivered Iranian FV4024 Chieftain ARVs derivatives for use with its **Khalid** fleet. The 56 000 kg combat weight Iranian/Jordanian FV4024 is based on the Chieftain Mk 5 chassis and is fitted with a hydraulically operated earth anchor and an Atlas crane unit.

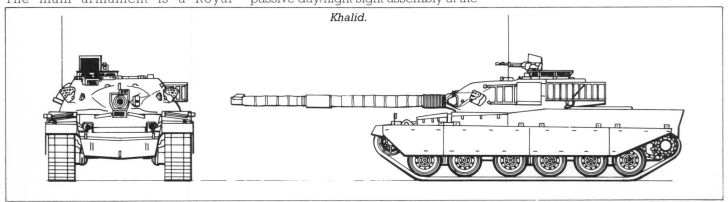

Khalid.

Specification:
First prototype: 1977
First production: 1981-1983 (274 built)
Current user: Jordan
Crew: 4
Combat weight: 58 000 kg
Ground pressure: 0.9 kg/cm²
Length gun forwards: 10.8 m
Width (with skirts): 3.52 m

Height (without AA gun): 3 m
Ground clearance: 0.51 m
Max. road speed: 50 km/h
Maximum range: 400 km
Fording: unprepared 1.1 m
Gradient: 60%
Side slope: 40%
Vertical obstacle: 0.91 m
Trench: 3.15 m

Powerpack: Perkins Engines (Shrewsbury) Condor V12-1200A liquid-cooled diesel developing 1200 hp and coupled to a David Brown Gear Industries TN37 automatic transmission
Armament: (main) 1 x 120 mm gun (64 rounds); (coaxial) 1 x 7.62 mm MG; (anti-aircraft) 1 x 7.62 mm MG; (smoke dischargers) 2 x 6

Khalid MBT of the Jordanian Army.

TR-77 (export)/TR-580/TR-800 (export)/TR-350   Romania

In the early seventies it is known that Romania approached a number of West German firms for aid in rebuilding her fleet of T-series MBTs to a more modern standard with new lengthened hull, suspension, running hear, engine and other components. To what extent any aid was given is not known but in 1977 the first Romanian T-55 variant, the **TR-580** (also variously known as the **TR-77** (its export designation), **M-77** (or US designation **M1977**), was seen.

This had all the features asked for by Romania including a lengthened rebuilt rear hull to accommodate a new 600 hp diesel powerpack. A number of the **TR-77** export models were sold to Egypt and Iraq, but the former country apparently returned many because of the poor standard of workmanship.

In the following year the **TR-85** (alternative designations **US M1978** and export **TR-800**) version was seen. This had many of the features of the **TR-580** but with a Chinese pattern 100mm rifled gun with thermal sleeve, a locally built Chinese Langzhou laser rangefinder module over the gun mantlet and a digital computerised fire control system. The turret was also completely new and the **TR-580** diesel engine exchanged for a more powerful 620 hp German model. A few export TR-800's were apparently sold to Iraq for use in the first Gulf War.

The final variant to-date to make its appearance is an upgrade package for the T-55A. This is offered for export only. The rebuild package can also be supplied in a kit form to export customers for local assembly. As far as it is known the only customer may have been Iraq, which is believed to have bought a number of kits during the first Gulf War to upgrade T-55 MBTs at its tank rebuild plant.

No support vehicle variants are known.

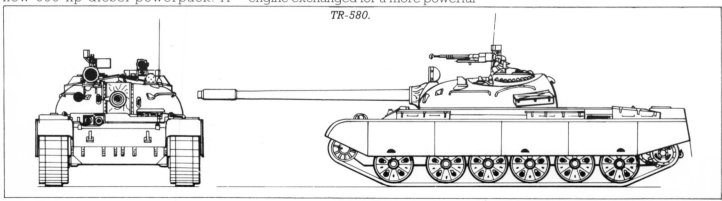

TR-580.

Specification:
First prototype: 1975-76
First production: 1977-1986
Current users: TR-77 Egypt, Iraq; TR-580 Romania; TR-800 Iraq; TR-850 Romania; T-55 rebuild – Iraq
Crew: 4
Combat weight: TR-77/TR-580 38 300 kg; TR-850/TR-800 43 500 kg
Ground pressure: n/av
Length gun forwards: 9.25 m

Width (over skirt): 3.3 m
Height (without AA gun): 2.4 m
Ground clearance: 0.43 m
Max. road speed: 65 km/h
Maximum range (with external tanks): 600 km
Fording: unprepared 1.2 m; prepared 5.5 m
Gradient: 60%
Side slope: 40%
Vertical obstacle: 0.8 m

Trench: 2.6 m
Powerpack: TR-77/TR-500 unidentified 600 hp diesel coupled to a manual transmission; TR-85/TR-800/T-55 rebuild unidentified 620 hp diesel coupled to a manual transmission
Armament: (main) 1 x 100 mm gun (40 plus rounds); (coaxial) 1 x 7.62 mm MG; (anti-aircraft) 1 x 12.7 mm MG; (smoke dischargers) 2 x 4 – 6

Romanian TR-580 MBT showing running gear from T-55 different and side skirts.

Olifant Mk 1A/Mk 1B   South Africa

The **Olifant (Elephant) Mk 1A** is an indigenous upgrade conversion of various Centurion MBT marks obtained by South Africa over the years. It is reminiscent of the original Israeli Sho't programme with improvements to firepower and mobility.

The main armament used is a locally built hybrid 105 mm rifled gun which uses the barrel of the British designed 105 mm L7A1 mated to the breech mechanism of the original 20 pdr OQF Mk 1 gun. Locally built HEAT, HESH, APDS-T, APFSDS-T and smoke ammunition types are carried.

The fire control system and sights are basically the original Centurion systems with the addition of a hand held laser rangefinder for the commander. For night fighting the gunner has an image intensifier assembly whilst the commander uses an infra-red/white light spotlight. The driver uses infra-red headlights.

The **Olifant Mk 1B** is effectively a total rebuild of the Mk 1A with the following features; lengthened hull; new engine, transmission and suspension; rebuilt turret with new stowage arrangement but same gun with thermal sleeve and integral fume extractor added; reduction in basic load rounds to 68; new driver's station; updated fire control system with ballistic computer and gunner's sight with integral laser rangefinder and new add-on special armour modules fitted to the turret front and sides, and hull glacis plate.

Other variants produced include an **ARV**, and **ARRV** which can carry and fit a complete powerpack unit and a Mk 1A or Mk 1B combat support version fitted with an Israeli type Track Width Mine Plough (TWMP) or mine-roller system.

Specification:
First prototype: Olifant Mk 1A 1972-3; Olifant Mk 1B 1986-7
First production: Olifant Mk 1A 1974-82 (about 300 conversions); Olifant Mk 1B 1991-current (complete rebuild of Mk 1A)
Current user: South Africa
Crew: 4
Combat weight: Olifant Mk 1A 56 000 kg; Olifant Mk 1B 58 000 kg

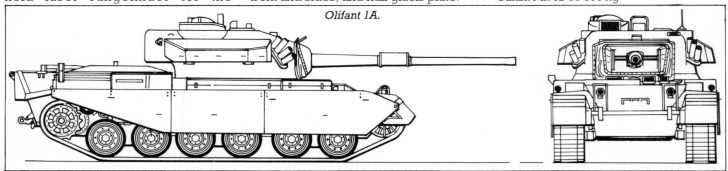
Olifant 1A.

Ground pressure: n/av
Length gun forwards: Olifant Mk 1A
9.83 m; Olifant Mk 1B 10.2 m
Width (with skirts): 3.38 m
Height (without AA gun): 2.94 m
Ground clearance: 0.5 m
Max. road speed: Olfant Mk 1A 45 km/h;
Olifant Mk 1B 58 km/h
Maximum range: 500 km

Fording: unprepared 1.2 m
Gradient: 60%
Side slope: 40%
Vertical obstacle: 0.9 m
Trench: 3.5 m
Powerpack: Olifant Mk 1A – V-12 air-cooled turbocharged diesel developing 750 hp coupled to an automatic transmission; Olifant Mk 1B – V-12 air-cooled

turbocharged diesel developing 850 hp coupled to an Amtra III automatic transmission
Armament: (main) 1 x 105 mm gun (Mk 1A – 72 rounds, Mk 1B – 68 rounds); (coaxial) 1 x 7.62 mm MG; (anti-aircraft) 1 x 7.62 mm MG; (smoke dischargers) 2 x 4

South African Defence ForceOliphant Mk 1A.

K1 (Type 88 or ROKIT) South Korea

The **K1 MBT** also known as the **Type 88** or **Republic of Korea Indigenous Tank (ROKIT)** was developed from 1979-84 by the US General Dynamics, Land Systems Division under contract to the South Korean government to meet a requirement for a locally built MBT suitable for use by the small stature South Korean personnel. Limited production began in 1985 and full series production in 1988. Three batches are believed to have been ordered – Block 1 210 vehicles, Block 2 325 vehicles and Block 3 316 vehicles with detail changes between each Block.

The low profile K1 uses a hybrid torsion/hydro-pneumatic suspension system and is armed with 105 mm M68A1 rifled gun that is fitted with fume extractor, thermal sleeve and Muzzle Reference System (MRS). The ammunition carried includes HEAT, APFSDS-T, HESH and smoke types.

The fire control system is based on a CDC modified M1 ballistic computer with an environmental sensor package and the gun's MRS. The commander has a French SFIM VS580-13 stabilised panoramic day sight assembly whilst the gunner has either, on Batch 1 & 3 vehicles, a stabilised Hughes Gunner's Primary sight (GPS) or, Batch 2 vehicles, a Texas Instruments stabilised Gunner's Primary Tank Thermal Sight (GPTTS) assembly. Weapon power control/turret stabilisation systems are Cadillac Gage Textron electro-hydraulic systems.

Armour protection is provided by both conventional steel armour plate and special armour configurations. An individual crew protection NBC system is installed.

The next generation K1 MBT is the **K1A1,** this will be armed with a 120 mm smoothbore gun, fire the same types of ammunition as the M1A1/M1A2 Abrams family and be fitted with full night vision equipment and a latest standard fire control

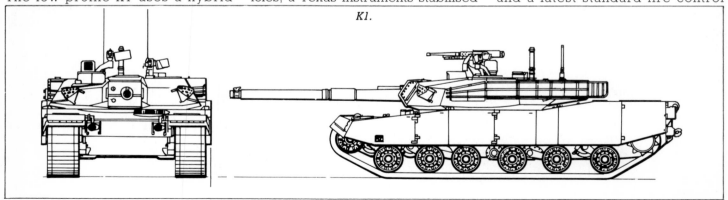

K1.

system. It is believe that the K1A1 is being developed as a response to a new North Korean MBT design possibly armed with a 125 mm gun system based on imported Russian/Chinese technology.

Vicker Defence Systems of the UK have designed a 22 mm length AVLB hydraulically launched scissors bridge system for use on the **K1** chassis whilst Krupp-MaK of Germany has developed an ARV variant with Hyundai. A total of 56 AVLBs have been ordered by the South Korean Army.

ARV variant of K-1 MBT chassis, the vehicle was developed by Hyundai in co-operation with the German firm MaK.

Specification:

First prototype: 1983
First production: 1985-current (over 600 built to-date)
Crew: 4
Combat weight: 52 000 kg
Ground pressure: n/av
Length gun forwards: 9.67 m
Width (with skirt): 3.59 m

Height (without AA gun): 2.25 m
Ground clearance: 0.46 m
Max. road speed: 65 km/h
Maximum range: 500 km
Fording: unprepared 1.2 m
Gradient: 60%
Side slope: 40%
Vertical obstacle: 1 m
Trench: 2.7 m

Powerpack:MTU MB 871 Ka-501 V-8 liquid-cooled turbocharged diesel developing 1200 hp coupled to a ZF LSG 3000 automatic transmission
Armament: (main) 1 x 105 mm gun (47 rounds); (coaxial) 1 x 7.62 mm MG; (anti-aircraft) 1 x 12.7 mm and 1 x 7.62 mm MGs; (smoke dischargers) 2 x 6

K1 MBT of the South Korean Army.

T-80 Series   Former Soviet Union

As the T-72 family increased in size the Soviets stopped production of the T-64 and switched their factories to production of the **T-80** model. Whilst derived from the T-64 and retaining that vehicles fully-stabilised 125 mm main gun and fire control system it also featured either a gas turbine or diesel engine, different suspension system, road wheels and tracks, and a smoother transmission.

In 1984 the T-80 began to appear in the Groups of Soviet Forces in Eastern Europe and by 1990 had almost totally supplanted the various T-64 variants in the Western and Northern Groups of Forces.

The fire control system includes a laser rangefinder, advanced ballistic computer, thermal sleeve on the gun barrel and a gun barrel warp sensor. The ammunition fired is the standard 125 mm family types – APFSDS-T, HE-FRAG(FS) and HEAT-FS – with the additional capacity for the AT-8 Songster radio command guided ATGW. The complete fire system allows targets out to 2500 metres to be effectively engaged by APFSDS-T ammunition and targets out to 4000 metres by the AT-8. The tank also has a limited shoot-on-the-move capability at low speeds. The gun uses a carousel-type autoloader with a 28-round capacity.

Beneath the glacis plate is a toothed dozer/plough with which the tank can dig its own fighting position within 15-20 minutes. It can also be fitted with KMT-5/6 mine roller/ploughs.

With the information release for the CIS talks the Russian Army designations for the T-80 variants have been discovered.

T-80 – initial production model with the features above.

T-80B – improved production model of T-80.

T-80BK – command version of T-80B with additional radio, second antenna on turret roof, land navigation system and no-ATGW capability.

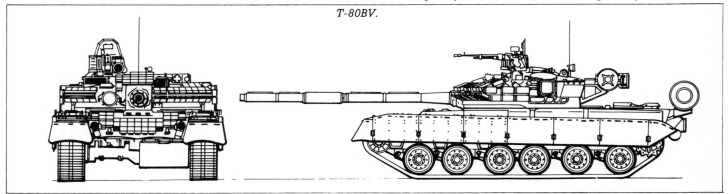

T-80BV.

T80 Series – continued

T-80D – further improved model of T-80/T-80B series.

T-80BV – the T-80B with bolts/brackets added all over the hull glacis and turret top, sides and front to take ERA boxes.

T-80BVK – command version of T-80BV with additional radio, second antenna and land navigation system.

T-80U – with either diesel or gas turbine engine, improved fire control system and laser designator/rangefinder assembly to accommodate the main gun fired semi-active laser guided AT-11 Sniper ATGW, redesigned turret with all-round advanced ERA protection, full length armoured side skirts and additional hull glacis plate with special armour slabs.

T-80UD - further improved model of T-80U.

As far as it is known the only vehicle built on the T-80 chassis to-date is the **152 mm 2S19 self-propelled gun system.**

Russian T-80/T-80B MBT fitted with gas turbine engine.

Specification:

First prototype: 1975-76

First production: 1979-current (18000 plus built)

Current users: Russia and CIS States

Crew: 3

Combat weight: 43 000 kg (45 000 kg T-80BV/T-80BVK, 46 000 kg T-80U/T-80UD)

Ground pressure: 0.93 kg/cm

Length gun forwards: 9.66 m

Width: 3.63 m

Height (without AA gun): 2.2 m

Ground clearance: 0.43 m

Max. road speed: 70 km/h

Maximum range (with external tanks): 440 km

Fording: unprepared 1.8 m; prepared 5.5 m

Gradient: 60%

Side slope: 40%

Vertical obstacle: 1.8 m

Trench: 2.95 m

Powerpack: T-80/T-80B series – multi-fuel gas turbine developing 1230 hp coupled to a manual transmission. Diesel versions also built. T-80U/T80UD diesel or gas turbine engine.

Armament: (main) 1 x 125 mm gun (37 rounds + 6 ATGW); (coaxial) 1 x 7.62 mm MG; (anti-aircraft) 1 x 12.7 mm MG; (smoke dischargers) 8-12 single

Russian T-80U medium tank with advanced ERA armour package.

T-72B/T-72S (export) series   Former Soviet Union

The T-72B and its variants was the main tank model used in the Soviet Central Group of Forces. The subsequent CFE talks revealed the following variants in use with the Russian and CIS armies.

T-72B – essentially a further development of the T-72A model with a number of modifications that includes a more powerful engine, improved armour protection and an upgraded fire control system to fire the AT-11 Sniper semi-laser guided ATGW. Radiation liners are fitted to the turret top, sides and rear.

T-72BK – command version of T-72B with additional radio, second antenna and land navigation system.

T-72B1 – identical to the T-72B but has no ATGW capability and is fitted with a different night sight in smaller armoured housing.

T-72BM – (or **Soviet Medium Tank (SMT) M1990**) is essentially an upgrading of the T-72 B design with a new style explosive reactive armour (ERA) package of single (hull glacis and turret front), double (turret sides and top) and triple (turret sides, front and top) layers of ERA blocks; bolt-on Kevlar fabric armour pieces over the top, sides and back of the turret rear half and crew hatches; additional armour plate welded to the glacis; and an enlarged turret with two shallow depressions either side of the gun with cavities that have been filled with replaceable improved special laminate armour inserts. The size of the modified turret has meant that the bottom edge of the front turret lobes has had to be cut away in order to allow the turret to rotate freely.

T-72S – export version of T-72B with AT-11 ATGW capability.

T-72S1 – further export version of T-72B with AT-11 ATGW capability.

The T-72B series carry the fully stabilised 125 mm 2A46 gun with the same light alloy thermal sleeve, bore evacuator and 22-round carousel-type autoloader of the other T-72 variants but carries 45 main 125 mm rounds (including the 6 AT-11 ATGW) instead of the earlier variants smaller basic load of conventional rounds. There is, however, a commensurate drop in the number of basic load rounds for the 7.62 mm PKT coaxial and 12.7 mm NVST anti-aircraft machine guns. The latter, unlike on the T-64 and T-80 MBTs, cannot be fired from under armour.

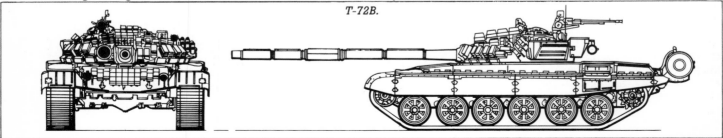

T-72B.

The T-72B models are also equipped with a PAZ radiation detection system and have an integral anti-radiation liner which has a secondary function as an anti-spall screen when the tank is hit by a kinetic energy (KE) or HESH round. A toothed dozer/plough is fitted below the glacis plate with which the tank can dig its own fighting position within 15-20 minutes. Like the T-64/T-80 and other T-62 variants the T-72B series can also be fitted with the KMT-5 mine roller set (three mine rollers and a central position plough) and/or the KMT-6 track mine plough assembly.

Specification:
First prototype: 1986-87
First production: 1988-current
Current users: Russia and CIS States
Crew: 3
Combat weight: 46 000 kg
(T-72BM 46 000 plus kg, T-72S 44 500 kg)
Ground pressure: n/av
Length gun forwards: 9.53 m
Width: 3.65 m
Height (without AA gun): 2.19 m
Ground clearance: 0.43 m
Max. road speed: 70 km/h
Maximum range (with external tanks): 640 km
Fording: unprepared 1.8 m; prepared 5.5 m

Gradient: 60%
Side slope: 40%
Vertical obstacle: 0.8 m
Trench: 2.8 m
Powerpack: Multi-fuel V-84 V-12 diesel developing 840 hp coupled to a manual transmission

Armament: (main) 1 x 125 mm gun (39 rounds + 6 ATGW); (coaxial) 1 x 7.62 mm MG; (anti-aircraft) 1 x 12.7 mm MG; (smoke dischargers) 1 x 8

Russian T-72B MBT equipped to fire the AT-11 Sniper.

T-72 A, G, M1 and PT-91 series   Former Soviet Union

The **T-72A/T-72M1** were the result of a mid seventies redesign of the basic T-72 model. This redesign was based around the availability of a new form of special armour that used ceramic elements in a laminated structure. The former Warsaw Pact allies, Czechoslovakia (now the Czech Republic and the Slovakian Republic) and Poland have produced their own versions of the T-72A.

A number of T-72A variants have been identified:

T-72A – first production model that also has the unofficial nickname of 'Dolly Parton'. The main differences from the earlier models are the incorporation of a gunner's sight with integral laser rangefinder, upgraded fire control system, the use of plastic armour side skirts and redesign of the cast steel turret that incorporate additional special laminate armour inserts in cavities either side of the main gun. External mounted radiation liners are also carried on turret top, sides and rear.

T-72G – Russian export version of T-72A. Built by Poland and Czechoslovakia under designation T-72M.

T-72AV – T-72A with explosive reactive armour package on turret, hull front and side skirts.

T-72AK – command tank version of T-72A with additional radio, second antenna and land navigation system.

T-72M1 – very similar to the T-72A in appearance but with no external turret radiation liners and slightly different glacis plate armour features. Also exported to a number of countries and license built by Poland, the former Czechoslovakia and India.

T-72M1K – command tank version of T-72M1 with additional radio, second antenna and land navigation system. Also built by Poland and Czechoslovakia.

PT-991 – the Polish Bumar-Labedy Machinery Industrial plant PT-91 Tvardy – (hard or rigid) medium tank has been developed for the Polish Army and export market. It is an upgraded version of the T-72M1 with a Polish designed and built computerised fire control system, new passive indigenous laminate armour and hull and turret single or double layer ERA protection packages, uprated 850 hp diesel engine with twice the T-72M1 range capability, laser warning receiver system and secondary weapon improvements.

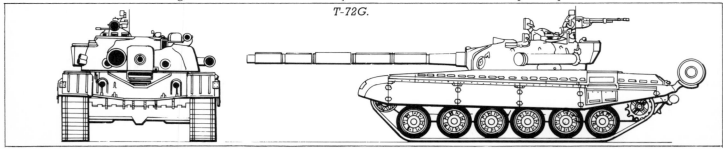

T-72G.

ZTS (Zavody Takeho Strojartva: Heavy Machinery Factory) Martin T-72 upgrade – the Slovakian Republic firm of ZTS Martin, which built the T-72M/T-72M1 for the former Czechoslovakian Army, is currently involved in the development of a modernised **T-72** variant for the home and export markets. No other details are available at present.

Specification:

First prototype: T-72A early 1970s; PT-91 1992

First production: former Soviet Union mid-seventies-current; Former Czechoslovakia (now Slovakian Republic (export T-72M/T-72M1) 1981-current; India (export T-72M1) 1987-current; Poland (export T-72M/T-72M1) 1981-current (1400 plus built)

Current users: Algeria (T-72G), Bulgaria (T-72G), CIS States, Cuba (T-72G),Czech Republic (T-72M/T-72M1), Finland (T-72G), Hungary (T-72G), India (T-72G/T-72M1), Iran (T-72M1), Iraq (T-72G/T-72M1), Libya (T-72G), Poland (T-72M/T-72M1), Russia, Serbia (T-72G), Slovakian Republic (T-72M/T-72M1), Syria (T-72G/T-72M1)

Crew: 3

Combat weight: 44 000 kg

Ground pressure: n/av

Length gun forwards: 9.53 m

Width: 3.59 m

Height (without AA gun): 2.19 m

Ground clearance: 0.43 m

Max. road speed: 60 km/h

Maximum range (with external tanks): 700 km

Fording: unprepared 1.2 m; prepared 5.5 m

Gradient: 60%

Side slope: 40%

Vertical obstacle: 0.8 m

Trench: 2.8 m

Powerpack: Multi-fuel V-46 V-12 diesel developing 780 hp and coupled to a manual transmission

Armament: (main) 1 x 125 mm gun (39 rounds); (coaxial) 1 x 7.62 mm MG; (anti-aircraft) 1 x 12.7 mm MG; (smoke dischargers) 12 single

Close-up of Russian T-72AV MBT showing ERA blocks fitted to glacis front, turret and side skirts.

T-72, A, B (export) and M series   Former Soviet Union

Developed in the late sixties the **T-72** was the standard tank successor to the T-55 MBT and by 1981 had largely replaced it on the Soviet tank factory production lines. It offers comparable protection and firepower capabilities to the T-64/80 models but is slower and less agile.

The fully stabilised 125 mm 2A46 Rapira 3 smoothbore gun uses a 22-round carousel-type autoloader that places the projectile and charge in the breech in a single movement. The system is difficult to reload and almost impossible to fire manually if it fails. A total of 39 main armament rounds are carried.

A number of early T-72 models have been noted.

T-72 (pre-production) – the pre-production model with T-64A gun/autoloader system. Most rebuilt with some of the later T-72M features.

T-72 – standard model built in several series. The T-72 has an optical coincidence rangefinder sight assembly on right of turret.

T-72A – export version of T-72. Not to be confused with later Former Soviet Army T-72A model.

T-72B – export version of late model T-72. Not to be confused with later Former Soviet Army T-72B model.

T-72K – command tank version of the T-72B with extra radio, second antenna on turret roof and land navigation system.

T-72M – upgraded T-72 with laser rangefinder assembly replacing coincidence rangefinder and increased main gun ammunition supply.

Support vehicles – A total of three support vehicles have been based on the T-72 chassis: the three-man 35 000kg **BREM-1** maintenance and recovery vehicle with a large hydraulic crane mounted on the left-hand side of the vehicle, a full-width dozer blade at the front and large cargo platform on the rear of the hull just behind the crew positions; **IMR-2 CEV** with front mounted variable shape dozer blade and centrally mounted hydraulically operated crane on the rear of the hull with various tool attachments; the two-man **MTU-72** armoured bridgelayer with a 20 m span foldable bridge.

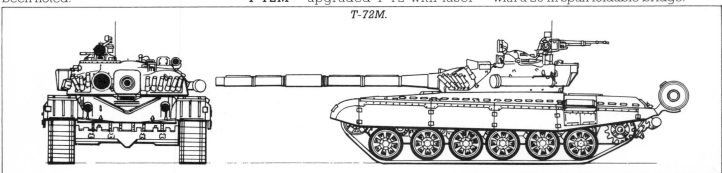

T-72M.

Specification:

First prototype: 1969-70
First production: former Soviet Union 1971-77
Current users: Bulgaria (T-72B), CIS, Hungary (T-72B), India (T-72B), Iraq (T-72B), Libya (T-72A/T-72B), Russia, Syria (T-72A/T-72B)
Crew: 3
Combat weight: 41 000 kg
Ground pressure: 0.83 kg/cm²

Length gun forwards: 9.53 m
Width: 3.46 m
Height (without AA gun): 2.19 m
Ground clearance: 0.43 m
Max. road speed: 60 km/h
Maximum range (with external tanks): 700 km
Fording: unprepared 1.2 m; prepared 5.5 m
Gradient: 60%
Side slope: 40%

Vertical obstacle: 0.8 m
Trench: 2.8 m
Powerpack: Multi-fuel V-46 V-12 diesel developing 780 hp and coupled to a manual transmission
Armament: (main) 1 x 125 mm gun (39 rounds); (coaxial) 1 x 7.62 mm MG; (anti-aircraft) 1 x 12.7 mm MG; (smoke dischargers) non (T-72M 1 x 12)

Russian T-72M MBT.

Originally fielded in 1967 the **T-64** did not reach the then groups of Soviet Forces in Eastern Europe in large numbers until 1974. The tank had a number of innovative design features including an autoloader with a 6-8 rpm rate of fire.

From the **T-64A** the gun main armament fitted is the fully stabilised 125 mm D81T Rapira 3 smoothbore gun that uses a rotating carousel magazine at the bottom of the turret basket. The 24 projectiles are stowed with their noses pointing in towards the centre with the propellant charges standing behind around the edge. A projectile must be lifted into position behind the breech with the propellant charge brought up behind it for the rammer to work. The system is difficult to reload and is almost impossible to manually fire if the autoloader fails for any reason.

The 12.7 mm NVST anti-aircraft machine gun can be fired from inside the turret. The tank is equipped with a PAZ radiation detector and has an integral anti-radiation/spall liner. Beneath the lower part of the glacis is a toothed dozer/plough with which the tank can dig its own fighting position within 15-20 minutes. It can also be fitted with KMT-5/6 mine roller/plough systems.

From the information released for the CIS talks the Russian designation of the T-64 variants have been identified.

T-64R – the original production model with a 115 mm D-68 gun and 40 rounds of ammunition. Of the ammunition carried 30 rounds were loaded in the autoloader. Distinguished by shorter barrel and no fume extractor, some 500 to 600 built.

T-64 – initial production vehicle with 125 mm D-81 gun. A total of 38 rounds carried. Most rebuilt to T-64A standard.

T-64A – with coincidence rangefinder (effective engagement range 1600 metres but built-in fire-control capacity available for 2200 metres). A total of 37 rounds are carried. A modified T-64A appeared in mid-seventies with

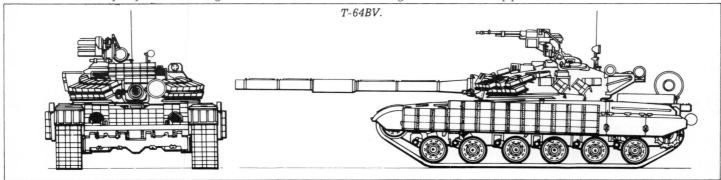

T-64BV.

addition of 2 x 6 smoke grenade launcher assemblies on each side of turret front.

T-64A Rebuilt – rebuild of T-64 and T-64A models. As T-64A but with addition of side skirts to improve hull side protection, glacis plate applique armour, new stowage arrangements and other minor changes.

T-64AK – command version of T-64 a with extra radio, second antenna on turret roof and land navigation system but no 12.7 mm NSVT machine gun at commander's station.

T-64B – redesigned T-64A, externally resembles the latter but with improved fire control system to accommodate 4000 m range AT-8 Songster ATGW (Russian name Kobra) and enhanced shoot-on-the-move capabilities. The missile's radio guidance box is on the left side of turret beneath the MG position. Also completely new second generation armour package. A total of 36 125 mm rounds and six Kobra missiles are carried. The T-64B was subsequently fitted with smoke dischargers.

T-64B1 – T-64B upgrade with further internal modifications.

T-64B1K – command version of T-64B1 with additional radio, second antenna on turret roof and land navigation system.

T-64BV – as T-64B but with bolts over turret and hull for mounting ERA package to give 25% increase in armour protection. Additional protection has also been fitted in the form of bolt-on Kevlar fabric armour pieces over the turret top, sides and rear.

T-64B1V – as T-64B1 but with modifications of the T-64BV to accommodate ERA package.

T-64B1VK – command version of T-64BV with additional radio, second antenna on turret roof and land navigation system.

As far as it is known no combat support vehicles have been built using the **T-64** chassis.

Specification:
First prototype: 1961-62
First production: 1965-1981 (13000 plus built)
Current users: Russia and other CIS states
Crew: 3
Combat weight: 38 000 kg (+1500 kg ERA T-64BV/T-64BV1K)
Ground pressure: 0.86 kg/cm^2
Length gun forwards: 9.24 m
Width (with skirts): 4.75 m
Height (without AA gun): 2.2 m
Ground clearance: 0.38 m
Max. road speed: 75 km/h
Maximum range (with external tanks): 600 km
Fording: unprepared 1.4 m; prepared 5.5 m
Gradient: 60%
Side slope: 40%
Vertical obstacle: 0.8 m
Trench: 2.7 m
Powerpack: 5 DTF 5-cylinder opposed-piston liquid-cooled diesel developing 750 hp coupled to a synchromesh hydraulically assisted transmission
Armament: (main) 1 x 125 mm gun (42 rounds); (coaxial) 1 x 7.62 mm MG; (anti-aircraft) 1 x 12.7 mm MG; (smoke dischargers) 2 x 6 (not T-64 Basic)

Russian T-64 MBT without any of the later upgrade modifications.

In an attempt to overcome some of the limitations of the T-55 the Soviets commenced quantity production of the **T-62** in 1962. The major difference was in the introduction of the 115 mm 2A20 Rapira smoothbore gun with a bore evacuator. The can fire HEAT-FS, HE-FRAG and APFSDS rounds at a maximum rate of 4 rpm. The flat trajectory of the APFSDS round coupled with the tank's stadia rangefinder means that a T-62 can effectively engage targets out to 1600 metres.

Although housed in a larger turret the 115 mm gun leaves little room for the crew so an automatic shell ejection system has to be added, this ejects spent shell cases out of a hatch in the turret rear. The system requires the gun to be elevated slightly during unloading with the power traverse shut off, thus limiting any rapid fire and second round hit capability. Also the ejection system must be perfectly aligned with the ejection port otherwise a spent shell case bounces around the inside of the turret.

The T-62 can create its own smoke-screen by injecting diesel fuel into its exhaust system. The tank is equipped with the PAZ radiation detection system and can use KMT-5/6 mine clearing gear.

The T-62 has seen combat in a number of wars including the 1973 Yom Kippur War, the 1982 Lebanon War, the 1980-88 First Gulf War, the 1990 Invasion of Kuwait and the 1991 Second Gulf War. In practically all these instances its combat record has not been exactly brilliant by any standards. Many examples of T-62 have turned up in the West and those captured by the Israelis have been modified to their own requirements as the Tirdan 6.

With the advent of the CFE treaty the Russian designations of a number of T-62 variants have been revealed.

T-62 Model 1960 – original prototypes in late fifties, 115 mm gun equipped trials batch in 1961 and series production from mid 1962 onwards.

T-62 Model 1967 – modernisation of

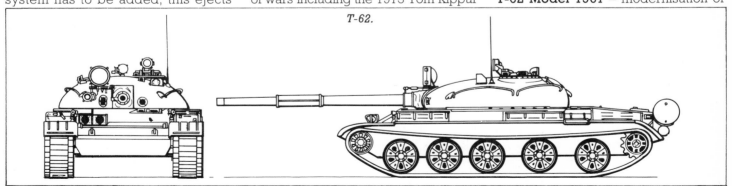

T-62.

initial production T-62 with reconfigured engine deck for easier access.

T-62K – command version T-62 with additional radio, 4 metre antenna and TNA-2 land navigation system. Only 37 rounds 115 mm ammunition carried.

T-62M Model 1972 – appeared in 1972 with modified turret carrying 12.7 mm DShK AA machine gun over new loader's rotating cupola position.

T-62M Model 1975 – the T-62M with KTD-1 box-type laser rangefinder over 115 mm gun.

T-62M Model 1984 – passive horseshoe shaped shields of homogeneous spaced armour fitted around the gun mantlet and turret sides frontal arc plus an optical belly armour package for mine protection. Developed especially for Afghanistan.

T-62M Model 1986 – fitted with the KTD-2 laser rangefinder, an upgraded diesel engine and the horseshoe armour package. Internally the vehicle is fitted with a ballistic computer fire control system to considerably improve the first round hit probability at 1600 metres range, a full weapon stabilisation system, night vision sights for gunner and commander, a laser guidance package for the 4000 m range 115 mm calibre Sheksna anti-tank missile and an improved model infra-red searchlight.

T-62MK – command version of T-62M variants with additional radio and land navigation system. Only 37 rounds 115 mm ammunition carried.

T-62MV – the T-62M Model 1986 fitted with Explosive Reactive Armour (ERA) boxes.

TO-62 – combat assault tank with 100m range coaxially mounted flame gun. Believed reduced 115 mm ammunition loaded to accommodate flame liquid reservoir.

IT-1 – short lived tank destroyer or 'fighter tank' variant trialled in the mid-sixties and subsequently built in small numbers in the late sixties. Armed with a single launcher unit that was raised through a turret mounted roof hatch for firing. A total of 15 missiles were carried. Proved useless in service with most being converted to other roles such as ARVs.

The North Koreans build a license-built version of the T-62 in underground production plants and have exported a number to Iran. They have significantly modified the design but accurate details are lacking at present.

The Iraqis also modified a number of their **T-62 Model 1962**, **T-62 Model 1967** and **T-62K** by fitting the loader's turret position with a DShK cupola ring from a T-55 MBT. These vehicles and later **T-62M** series versions were also provided with sheet metal protective covers for the 800 m range Luna L-2G infra-red/whitelight searchlight that is mounted coaxially to the right of the main gun and the commander's OU-3G infra-red searchlight mounted at the front of his cupola. A number of vehicles also had Chinese-type sand shields added to their sides.

Specification:
First prototype: 1957-58
First production: Soviet Union 1961-1975 (20 000 built), Czechoslovakia 1973-1978 (1500 built for export), North Korea late seventies-current (700 plus built)
Current users: Afghanistan, Algeria, Angola, Bulgaria, Cuba, Egypt, Ethiopia, Iran, Iraq, Israel (Tirdan 6), North Korea, Libya, Mongolia, Syria, Russia and CIS States, Vietnam, Republic of Yemen
Crew: 4
Combat weight: 40 000 kg (plus 3900 kg horseshoe armour weight T-62M Model 1984 onwards)
Ground pressure: 0.77 kg/cm^2
Length gun forwards: 9.34 m
Width: 3.3 m
Height (with AA gun): 2.4 m
Ground clearance: 0.43 m
Max. road speed: 60 km/h

Maximum range (with external tanks): 650 km
Fording: unprepared 1.4 m; prepared 5.5 m
Gradient: 60%
Side slope: 30%

Vertical obstacle: 0.8 m
Trench: 2.9 m
Powerpack: V-55-5 V-12 liquid-cooled diesel developing 580 hp coupled to a manual transmission

Armament: (main) 1 x 115 mm gun (40 rounds); (coaxial) 1 x 7.62 mm MG; (anti-aircraft) 1 x 12.7 mm MG (T-62M series)

Captured Iraq T-62 medium tank on display in Kuwait, mid 1992.

T-55   Former Soviet Union

The **T-55** evolved in the late fifties to meet a Soviet Army requirement for a MBT model that could survive and fight on the nuclear battlefield. The main changes from the T-54B that it was based on involved the deletion of the large vent dome cover by the loader's turret hatch, a new model loader's hatch which fitted the flush to the turret roof, an uprated engine and transmission, a partial turret basket floor with increased ammunition stowage capacity and the use of an improved NBC sealing arrangement with a partial PAZ radiation detection system. The main armament used is the two-plane stabilised 100 mm D-10T2S rifled gun. The ammunition types available are the same as for the T-54 –

namely APC-T, AP-T, HEAT-FS, HVAPDS-T, HE and FRAG-HE. Effective engagement range with the gunner's stadiametric rangefinder is limited to 1000 metres.

Also the tank cannot effectively fire-on-the-move at any speed so has to fire either from the short halt or dedicated defensive fighting position.

A number of variants were identified over the years from Soviet/Russian sources. These are:

T-55 Model 1958 – initial production version as described in the text above.

T-55A – introduced about 1960 with final deletion of bow MG and fitting of internal turret radiation/spall liner and full PAZ system.

T-55A Model 1970 (or **T-55AM**) –

T-55A fitted with 12.7 mm DShK anti-aircraft machine gun and position. Subsequently refitted to earlier T-55 and T-55A models.

T-55 Model 1974 – T-55 models refitted with KTD-2 laser rangefinder in armoured housing over main gun.

T-55K – three command tank version of T-55 model 1958 with various additional communications equipment and a reduced basic load of 37 rounds. Designations are **T-55K1, T-55K2** and **T-55K3**.

T-55AK – command tank version of T-55A with additional radio and reduced basic load.

OT-55 – combat engineer assault version of T-55 Model 1958 with 200 m range ATO-200 flame gun mounted in

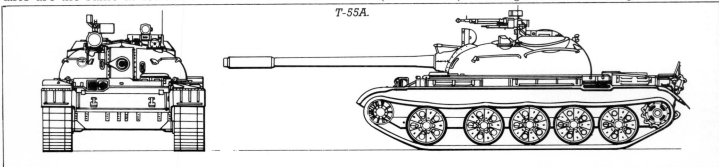
T-55A.

lieu of coaxial machine gun and a reduced basic load of some 20-25 rounds. Used by Syria and Egypt in 1973 Yom Kippur War.

Support vehicles – a wide variety of specialist support vehicles have either been produced on or converted from the T-55 chassis. These include the **BTS-2**, **WZT-1**, **BTS-3**, **BTS-4**, **MT-55**, **WZT-2** and **WPT-2 ARVs**, the **MTU-20**, **BLG-60**, **BLG-60M**, **MTU-3** and **MT-55 AVLBs**, the **IWT** and **IMR combat engineer vehicles** and the **T-55A/PW-LWD**, **T-55/KMT-4**, **T-55/KMT-4M**, **T-55/KMT-5**, **T-55/KMT-5M**, **T-55/PT-54**, **T-55/PT-54M** and **T-55/PT-55 mine-clearing vehicles**. There are also the **T-55/BTU** and **T-55/BTU-55 dozer blade tanks**.

Specification:
First prototype: 1956-57
First production: Soviet Union 1958-81 (27 500 built), Czechoslovakia 1964-73 (5000 built), Poland 1960-72 (5000 built)
Current users: Approximately 55 countries and guerrilla/militia armed forces use the T-54/T-55 MBT famliy
Crew: 4
Combat weight: 36 000 kg
Length gun forwards: 9.0 m
Width: 3.27 m
Height (without AA gun): 2.4 m
Ground clearance: 0.43 m

Max. road speed: 50 km/h
Maximum range (with external tanks): 715 km
Fording: unprepared 1.4 m; prepared 4.6 m
Gradient: 60%
Side slope: 40%
Vertical obstacle: 0.8 m
Trench: 2.7 m

Powerpack: V-55 V-12 liquid-cooled diesel developing 580 hp coupled to a manual transmission
Armament: (main) 1 x 100 mm gun (43 rounds); (coaxial) 1 x 7.62 mm MG; (bow) 1 x 7.62 mm MG (T-55 only); (anti-aircraft) 1 x 12.7 mm MG (T-55A onwards)

T-55A of former Czechoslovakian Army.

The **T-54** was designed during the latter stages of the Second World War as the T-34-85 successor. It uses the 100 mm D-10 series rifled tank gun with a gunner's stadiametric rangefinder to effectively engage targets out to 1000 metres range. The vehicle can also produce its own smokescreen by injecting diesel oil into its exhaust system.

The Czechoslovakian and Polish built **T-54s**, like their later T-55 and T-72 models, are considered to be built to a significantly higher standard than the comparable Soviet built models. The T-54 can be fitted with a 3.4 m wide BTU or 3.8 m wide BTU-55 bulldozer blades.

Over the years a number of variants have been identified:

T-54 – built between 1946-1951 in several series differing in external and internal details to progressively overcome vehicle deficiencies. The basic T-54 series include the T-54 Model 1946 (prototype series), T-54 Model M 1949 (first mass production version) and T-54 Model 1951. The latter with its classic half egg-cup turret shape was adopted as the definite configuration for the T-54/55 family. The main gun armament used was the non-stabilised 100 mm D-10T rifled gun. With later model features added after rebuilding the designation changed to **T-54M**.

T-54A Model 1951 – prototyped in 1951 it was introduced into service in 1964 with the single axis stabilised D-10T main gun and fume extractor,

OPVT deep fording snorkel equipment for crossing rivers underwater, driver's infra-red night driving equipment and five-spoke road wheels. The Chinese built this under license as the Type 59.

T-54B Model 1952 – prototyped in 1952 and initially introduced into limited service in 1955. Fitted with two-axis stabilised 100 mm D-10T2S main gun, a new full active infra-red night fighting system and full electric turret power traverse. Polish-built version designated T-54AM.

T-54K – command tank version of T-54.

T-54BK – command tank version of T-54B.

TO-54 – combat engineer flame-thrower tank version of T-54 with 160m range ATO-1 flame gun replacing co-

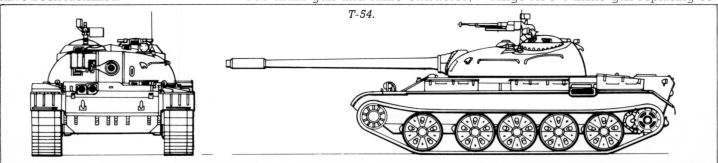

T-54.

axial machine gun.

ZSU-57-2 – built from 1951-1963 as self-propelled AA gun with twin 57 mm S-68 cannon and optical sighting equipment in an open turret mounted on a lightened T-54 chassis.

ZSU-122-54 – Assault gun/tank destroyer version built in limited numbers from 1949 onwards through the fifties on T-54 chassis, armed with a 122 mm D-49S gun, two 14.5 mm heavy machine guns and fitted with a commander's optical rangefinder sighting system.

Support vehicles – a number are based on or use the **T-54** chassis: the **BTS-1 ARV**, the **MTU-1 AVLB** and the **T-54/PT-3, T-54/PT-54, T-54/PT-54M, T-54/PT-55, T-54/KMT-4, T-54/KMT-4M, T-54/KMT-5** and **T-54/KMT-5M mine clearing vehicles.** Plus the **T-54/BTU** and **T-54/BTU-55 dozer tanks.**

Specification:

First prototype: 1945

First production: Soviet Union 1946-1958 (35 000 built), Czechoslovakia 1958-1964 (2 500 built), Poland 1956-1964 (3 000 built)

Current users: Approximately 55 countries and guerrilla/militia armed forces use the T-54/55 BMT family

Crew: 4

Combat weight: 36 000 kg

Length gun forwards: 9 m

Width: 3.27 m

Height (without AA gun): 2.4 m

Ground clearance: 0.43 m

Max. road speed: 50 km/h

Maximum range (with external tanks): 600 km

Fording: unprepared 1.4 m; prepared 4.6 m

Gradient: 60%

Side slope: 40%

Vertical obstacle: 0.8 m

Trench: 2.7 m

Powerpack: V-54 V-12 liquid-cooled diesel developing 500 hp and coupled to a manual transmission

Armament: (main) 1 x 100 mm gun (34 rounds); (coaxial) 1 x 7.62 mm MG; (bow) 1 x 7.62 mm MG; (anti-aircraft) 1 x 12.7 mm MG

T-54 of Angolan Army.

T-34-85 **Former Soviet Union**

By the end of the Second World War the **T-34-85** was the standard medium tank of the Soviet Army. Its origins lay in the capture of a German Army Tiger I tank in 1943 when the Soviet Army decided on a major upgrading of its T-34-76 tank with a new larger 85 mm calibre weapon capable of defeating both the armour of the Tiger and that of the forthcoming German Panther tank. After a successful war career the T-34-85 continued in production, initially in the Soviet Union and then its two major Warsaw Pact allies, until the late fifties and was widely exported. It has seen combat service in numerous wars such as Korea and the Middle East conflicts and was still being met in combat during the eighties by Israel during its

1982 Lebanon war, South Africa during its various incursions into Angola, and in the early nineties in the various Yugoslavian wars.

The following Russian production variants have been identified:

T-34-85 (M1943) – initial production model with modified 85 mm D-5T gun of KV-85.IS-1 and SU-85 and PTK-5 MK-4 periscopes.

T-34-85 (M1944) – standard production model with definitive 85 mm ZiS S-53 gun and MK-4 periscopes. The tanks were built with three variations in cast turret configurations – flattened, composite and angle-jointed. There were also a number of external configuration changes.

T-34-85 (M1947) – with improved V-2-

34M engine, new sights, communications gear and other minor modifications.

T-34-85M – in the late sixties several thousand Soviet mobilisation reserve T-34-85 were rebuilt with 520 hp V-54 diesel engines, T-55 style road wheels and numerous internal changes. Some were then exported and have been noted in combat in Angola, Vietnam and during the 1973 Yom Kippur War. Many of the export T-34-85 users have also fitted a 12.7 mm DShKM AA MG to the turret roof for use by the tank commander. Although a large number of support vehicle conversions are known to have been made none are believed to be in service today.

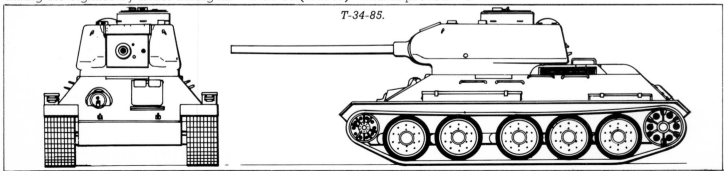

T-34-85.

Specification:
First prototype: 1943
First production: Soviet Union 1944-1950
(44 000 built), Czechoslovakia 1951-1958
(3000 built), Poland 1951-1957 (1400 built)
Current users: Approximately 32 countries
and guerrilla forces still use this vehicle
Crew: 5
Combat weight: 32 000 kg
Ground pressure: 0.83 kg/cm²
Length gun forwards: 8.08 m
Width: 3 m
Height: 2.74 m
Ground clearance: 0.38 m
Max. road speed: 55 km/h
Maximum range (with external tanks):
310 km
Fording: unprepared 1.3 m
Gradient: 60%
Side slope: 40%
Vertical obstacle: 0.73 m
Trench: 2.5 m
Powerpack: V-2-34M or V-2-34 V-12
liquid-cooled diesel engine developing
500 hp and coupled to a manual
transmission
Armament: (main) 1 x 85 mm gun
(56 rounds); (coaxial) 1 x 7.62 mm MG;
(bow) 1 x 7.62 mm MG

T-34-85 in US Army service as Opposing Forces training vehicle in mid- eighties.

103

Bofors **Stridsvagn** (Strv) **103A/B/C**   **Sweden**

The **Strv 103** (or **Bofors S-tank**) is the only turretless MBT in operational service in the world. The fixed 105 mm L74 rifled gun is laid in elevation/depression by tilting the hull via a hydropneumatic suspension system and in azimuth by turning the whole vehicle using only its tracks. The ammunition types used include APFSDS-T, APDS, HESH and smoke.
Three versions have been produced to-date:

Strv 103A – the original production batch with no flotation screen (to allow amphibious operations at max waterspeed of 6 km/h) nor integral under glacis dozer blade. All upgraded to Strv 103B standard.

Strv 103B – standard production model with flotation screen assembly and integral dozer blade beneath the glacis plate to enable vehicle to dig its own fighting positions.

Strv 103C – the Strv 103B model upgrade between 1986-1989 with new Detroit Diesel engine, modified transmission and modern computerised fire control system with a gunner's integral laser rangefinder sighting assembly. All Strv 103 models were fitted for an NBC system but do not carry one. The Strv 103C has its own dozer blade that folds back under the nose of the tank for digging defensive positions.

The only combat support version fielded to-date is a **mine-clearing vehicle** which is an Strv-103 fitted with the locally designed and built 6000 kg Minvalt mine-roller system.

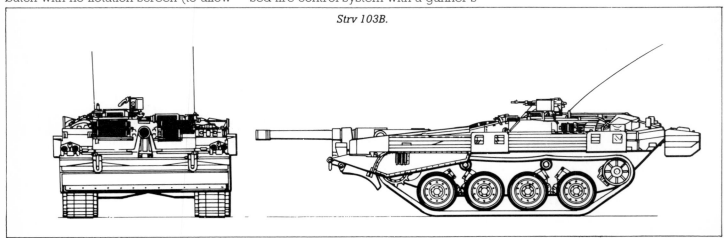

Strv 103B.

Specification:
First prototype: Strv 103 1961, Strv 103C 1982-83
First production: Strv 103A/B 1966-71 (300 built, Strv 103C rebuilt from Strv 103B 1986-89)
Current user: Sweden
Crew: 3
Combat weight: Strv 103A 39 000 kg; Strv 103B 39 700 kg; Strv 103C 42 500 kg
Ground pressure: Strv 103A 0.85 kg/cm²; Strv 103B 1.04 kg/cm²; Strv 103C 1.17 kg/cm²

Length gun forwards: 9 m
Width: Strv 103A 3.4 m; Strv 103B/C 3.6 m
Height (without AA gun): 2.14 m
Ground clearance: 0.4 m
Max. road speed: 50 km/h
Maximum range: 400 km
Fording: unprepared 1.5 m
Gradient: 60%
Side slope: 40%
Vertical obstacle: 0.9 m
Trench: 2.3 m
Powerpack: Strv 103A/B Rolls Royce K60 diesel developing 240 hp with a Boeing 553 gas turbine developing 490 hp for combat boost, both coupled to Bofors automatic transmission; Strv 103C – Detroit Diesel 6V-53T diesel developing 290 hp with a Boeing 553 gas turbine developing 490 hp for combat boost, both coupled to a Bofors automatic transmission
Armament: (main) 1 x 105 mm gun (50 rounds); (coaxial) 2 x 7.62 mm MG; (anti-aircraft) 1 x 7.62 mm MG; (smoke dischargers) 8 single; (target illumination) 2 x 71mm Bofors Lyran

Latest variant of Swedish Army S-tank, the Strv-103C.

Pz 68 series

The **Pz 68** is the evolutionary development model of the Pz 61 design built in four differing series. Compared to its predecessor it has a full gun stabilisation system for the same rifled 105 mm main armament as the Pz 61, an improved external turret stowage arrangement, a deep fording capability (with preparation to 2.3 m), uprated MTU MB 837 diesel engine and modified transmission and running gear assemblies. A total of 56 rounds are carried and the main gun is fitted with a fume evacuator.

The four series built are:

Pz 68 Series 1 – as described in the text with a total of 170 procured between 1971-74.

Pz 68 Series 2 – a total of 60 built in 1977 with uprated electrical supply, improved air filter system to remove carbon monoxide and a thermal sleeve for the 105 mm gun.

Pz 68 Series 3 – 110 built 1978-79 with a larger cast turret and all the improvements found on the Series 2 vehicle.

Pz 68 Series 4 – much reduced order of 60 (from intended 170) delivered 1983-84. Essentially equivalent to the Series 3 batch but with several minor modifications.

Pz 68/88 – all the Pz 68 Series 3 and 4 vehicles plus the 25 best condition Series 2 vehicles have undergone a major upgrading programme during the early nineties. This included the fitting of a computerised fire control system with a gunner's gyrostabilised sighting unit and integral laser range-finder module (to replace the current gunner's coincidence rangefinder system), a locally designed and built Muzzle Reference System, improved suspension and a collective crew NBC system.

The combat support vehicles based on the Pz 68 chassis are included in the Pz 61 entry.

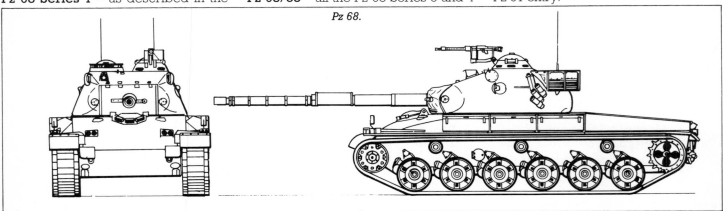

Pz 68.

Specification:

First prototype: 1968
First production: 1971-1984 (in four series totalling 390 tanks)
Current user: Switzerland
Crew: 4
Combat weight: 39 700 kg
Ground pressure: 0.86 kg/cm²
Length gun forwards: 9.5 m
Width: 3.14 m
Height (without AA gun): 2.75 m
Ground clearance: 0.41 m
Max. road speed: 55 km/h
Maximum range: 350 km
Fording: unprepared 1.1 m
Gradient: 60%
Side slope: 40%
Vertical obstacle: 0.8 m
Trench: 2.6 m
Powerpack: MTU MB 837 Ba-500 V-8 supercharged liquid-cooled diesel development 660 hp and coupled to an SLM semi-automatic transmission
Armament: (main) 1 x 105 mm gun (56 rounds); (coaxial) 1 x 7.5 mm MG; (anti-aircraft) 1 x 7.5 mm MG; (smoke dischargers) 2 x 3; (illumination) 2 x 71 mm Bofors Lyran

Swiss Army Pz 68 Series 4 MBT.

Pz 61   Switzerland

The **Pz 61** was the first Swiss indigenously designed MBT to be placed into operational service. The vehicle has an NBC system and is fitted with the locally produced and modified Panzer Kanone 61 (Pz Kan 61) version of the Royal Ordnance 105 mm L7 series rifled gun. This fires HE, HESH, APDS, smoke and APFSDS-T rounds and uses a gunner's coincidence rangefinder.

The coaxial armament originally fitted is the 20 mm Oerlikon cannon model 5TGK with 240 rounds of mixed round types such as AP-T, SAPHEI, SAPHEI-T, HEI and HEI-T. A 7.5 mm Model 51 machine gun is fitted to the loader's hatch for anti-aircraft use.

All Pz 61 MBTs are expected to be withdrawn from service in the mid-nineties. Over the years the Pz 61 has been modified several times. The following are the identified sub-variants:

Pz 61 models AA7/AA8 – the basic Pz 61 fitted in 1976/7 period with improved maintenance access facilities, a new radio and a dry air filter to improve the reliability of the installed electronics.

Pz 61 model AA9 – this is the latest modification standard with all the features of the AA7/8 models and the 20 mm coaxial cannon replaced by a 7.5 mm machine gun.

AVLB and **ARV** prototypes using the Pz 61 MBT chassis were developed in the late sixties but were eventually produced on the later Pz 68 chassis. These variants are respectively designated the **Bruckenlegepanzer 68** (**Bru Pz 68**) – 30 vehicles produced between 1974-77 – and the **Entpannungspanzer 65** (**Entp Pz 65**) – 69 vehicles produced between 1970-78.

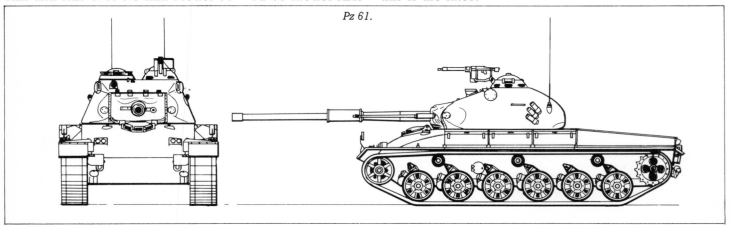

Pz 61.

Specification:

First prototype: 1960-61
First production: 1965-1966 (i150 built)
Current user: Switzerland
Crew: 4
Combat weight: 38 000 kg
Ground pressure: 0.85 kg/cm²
Length gun forwards: 9.43 m
Width: 3.1 m
Height (without AA gun): 2.72 m
Ground clearance: 0.42 m
Max. road speed: 55 km/h
Maximum range: 300 km
Fording: unprepared 1.1 m
Gradient: 60%
Side slope: 40%
Vertical obstacle: 0.8 m
Trench: 2.6 m
Powerpack: MTU MB 837 Ba-500 V-8 supercharged liquid-cooled diesel developing 630 hp and coupled to an SLM semi-automatic transmission
Armament: (main) 1 x 105 mm gun (52 rounds); (coaxial) 1 x 20 mm cannon (Pz 61), 1. 7.5 mm MG (Pz 61 model AA9); (anti-aircraft) 1 x 7.5 mm MG, (smoke dischargers) 2 x 3; (illumination) 2 x 71 mm Bofors Lyran

Right: Swiss Army Pz 65 ARV member of Pz 61/Pz 68 family, built on Pz 68 chassis.

Below: Swiss Army Pz 61 MBT AA9 variant.

Vickers Defence Systems **Challenger 2** **UK**

The Vickers Defence Systems **Challenger 2** is the British designed and built winner of the British Army's Staff Requirement (Land) 4026 replacement programme for the remaining Chieftain MBT fleet. The other contenders were the American M1A2 Abrams, the German Leopard 2 (Improved) and the French Leclerc.

The Challenger 2 was developed under a UK MoD 'proof-of-principle' fixed price phased contract which involved the production of nine prototype tanks and two additional turrets to demonstrate that it can fully meet the operational requirements laid down and be produced to the specified production standard at a previously stated cost. The initial contract for 127 Challenger 2 MBTs plus 13 **Challenger 2 Driver Training** tanks was placed in June 1991.

The hull and powerpack are similar to that used in Challenger 1 but the transmission, hydro-pneumatic suspension and running gear are to a higher standard than the Challenger Improvement Programme (CHIP)

requirements.

The major change is the use of a completely redesigned turret, made with second generation Chobham laminated special armour and fitted with the high pressure 120 mm L30 CHARM 1 rifled gun system firing APFSDS-T (the depleted uranium CHARM 3 Kinetic Energy projectile type for use against both special passive and ERA armour), HESH and smoke rounds.

It is also fitted with a state-of-the-art fire control system based on the CDC Mission Management Computer

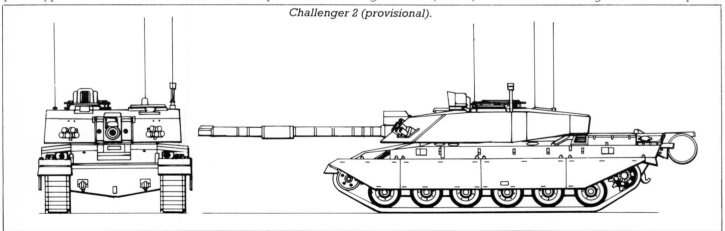

Challenger 2 (provisional).

One of the Challenger 2 prototypes showing commander's VS580 roof sight and TOGS over the 120mm L30 main gun.

System, a joint SAGEM/Vickers Defence Systems SAMS stabilised gunner's sight system with integral carbon dioxide laser rangefinder, a SFIM model VS580 commander's gyro-stabilised day sight assembly with integral laser rangefinder, a separate Barr and Stroud thermal imaging TOGS surveillance sighting system mounted in a protected box over the main gun for display to the gunner and commander's positions on individual monitors distinct from their sights and the built-in capacity for future fitting of the Battlefield Information Control System (BICS).

The British Army is equipping two regiments with the Challenger 2. The first is to be fielded in 1995 and will comprise a Regimental HQ (with two MBTs) and three squadrons (each of four three vehicle troups). The Regimental total of 38 Challenger 2s is a significant reduction when compared to current regimental totals of 43 or 57 MBTs. It is probable that the six regiments of Challenger 1 MBTs may also be replaced by Challenger 2s. If correct then a further order for 249 will be placed to extend production beyond 1998. Part of the first Challenger 2 order was for the only support tank variant to-date, a Driver Training tank model.

In early 1993 Oman placed an order for Challenger 2s to replace its existing Chieftain fleet. The initial order is for 18 Challenger 2s, two Driver Training tanks and four support Challenger 1 ARRVs, The order also included four Alvis Stormer APCs and nine Unipower M series tank transporters. An option was also apparently placed on a repeat Challenger 2 order of 18 vehicles to be actioned at a later date.

Specification:
First prototype: 1989
First production: 1993 (initial order for 127 placed in 1991 for British Army with first deliveries 1994, order for 18 Challenger 2 MBTs + option on further 18 placed in 1993 by Oman, further British Army order likely for 259)
Crew: 4
Combat weight: 62 500 kg
Ground pressure: 0.9 kg/cm^2
Length gun forwards: 11.55 m
Width: 3.52 m
Height (without AA gun): 2.49 m
Ground clearance: 0.5 m
Max. road speed: 57 km/h
Maximum range: 400 km
Fording: unprepared 1.1 m
Gradient: 60%
Side slope: 40%
Vertical obstacle: 0.9 m
Trench: 2.35 m

Powerpack: Perkins Engines (Shrewsbury) Condor CV12TCA liquid-cooled diesel developing 1200 hp and coupled to a David Brown Gear Industries TN54 automatic transmission
Armament: (main) 1 x 120 mm gun (52 rounds); (coaxial) 1 x 7.62 mm MG; (anti-aircraft) 1 x 7.62 mm MG; (smoke dischargers) 2 x 5

Challenger 2 prototype firing.120mm L30 rifled gun at night.

Vickers Defence Systems Challenger 1 UK

The **Challenger 1** MBT is an evolutionary derivative of the Shir 2 MBT originally developed for the Shah of Iran's Army but subsequently cancelled by the Islamic Republic of Iran before any production could be undertaken. Compared to the Chieftain MBT is has a more powerful diesel engine, new transmission, improved suspension and extensive use of Chobham laminated special armour in the construction of the hull and turret. The latter feature gives the vehicle a distinctive slab-sided appearance.

The Challenger was produced in a number of versions, including the **Challenger 1 Mk 1**, **Challenger Mk 2** and **Challenger 1 Mk 3**. Each introducing additional features to the vehicle.

The main armament used is the 120 mm L11A5 rifled gun with thermal sleeve, fume extractor and a muzzle reference system. But this is being replaced by the 120 mm L30 Challenger Armament (CHARM) production variant of the high pressure rifled Royal Ordnance Nottingham/DRA RARDE Modern Technology Gun family. The ammunition fired is of the two-piece type and includes APDS-T (not for L30), APFSDS-T (with a depleted uranium CHARM version available for the L30 gun), HESH, smoke and various training variants. A total of 64 projectile and 42 charge stowage positions are available, with the latter capable of taking either one discarding sabot charge or two smoke/HESH charges.

The fire control system is similar to that used in the Chieftain – the Marconi Radar and Control System Improved Fire Control System (IFCS) – with the gunner and commander having separate monitor displays for the Barr and Stroud Thermal Observation and Gunnery Sight (TOGS) system fitted.

The only combat support vehicle produced to-date on the Challenger 1 chassis is the **ChallengeR Armoured Repair and Recovery Vehicle (CRARRV)**. A total of 80 production standard **CRARRVs** are being delivered from 1990 onwards for use with the REME detachment on the seven Challenger 1 Regiments in the British Army.

All Challenger 1 MBTs are fitted for the Pearson Combat Dozer Blade and at

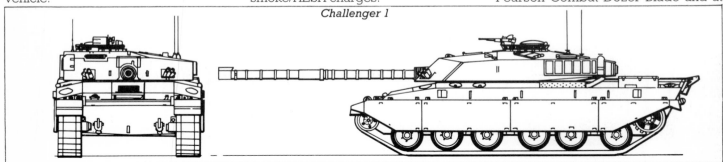

Challenger 1

Challenger 1s of British Army upgraded to Challenger 1 Mk 3 standard for use in Operation Desert Storm.
Note kit stowage around turret, additional passive armour for side skirts and rear mounted 200 litre fuel tanks.

least one vehicle in each armoured squadron carries the equipment.

In 1989-90 a total of 17 **Driver Training tanks** were produced for the British Army. The training vehicle is essentially the Challenger 1 MBT chassis fitted with a non-rotating turret configured for the instructor role.

The British Army has trialled a **Challenger Improvement Programme (CHIP),** but is more likely to procure additional Challenger 2s than procure it.

For the Gulf War three regiments of Challenger 1 were deployed to Saudi Arabia for use with the First (British) Armoured Division: 14th/20th King's Hussars (43 Challenger 1, attached to 4th Armoured Brigade); The Royal Scots Dragoon Guards (57 Challenger 1, attached to 7th Armoured Brigade): and The Queens Royal Irish Hussars (57 Challenger 1, attached to 7th Armoured Brigade). In addition further Challengers were assigned to the Armoured Brigades and Armoured Division as HQ vehicles and battlefield replacements, the latter including the Divisional assigned Armoured Delivery Group (ADG) with three full squadrons of War Maintenance Reserve Challengers crewed by the Life Guards.

The ADG totalled some 250 vehicles with approximately 1200 men, and followed in the immediate rear of the Armoured Brigades ready to commit as required reserves ranging from a single tank to a full sized battle group. Over 200 Challenger 1's were sent to the Gulf together with the first 12 production CRARRVs to support the MBTs.

Because of the very nature of the desert battlefield and the Iraqi threat anti-armour capabilities a Challenger Uparmouring programme was undertaken. This involved the production of special Vickers Defence Systems passive skirt armour kits for the hull sides and an add-on Royal Ordnance Explosive Reactive Armour (ERA) package for the bow toe plate and glacis region. The complete armour upgrading added several thousand kilogrammes to the Challenger's basic combat weight but did not adversely affect its battlefield performance.

Other improvements included: the use of the interim Jericho 2 Depleted Uranium APFSDS round by taking the L26A1 Charm 1 projectile of the CHARM programme and marrying it with an L14 lower pressure charge to increase accuracy and penetration; the enhancing of all the MK 2 variant Challengers present in the Gulf to the latest Mk 3 standard; the fitting of various equipment to make Challenger fully capable of extended operations in desert conditions; the addition of external fittings to allow the vehicles to carry two 200 litre fuel tanks at the rear; and the addition of a device to a number of Challengers in order to give them the capability of laying down a protective 'tail smokescreen' by pumping atomised diesel fuel into the tank's exhaust system.

Most of the improvement work and fitting of add-on packages was performed in the Gulf region by the REME and various equipment manufacturer's engineers.

All these improvements worked as not one Challenger 1 nor any of its crewmen were lost in combat. The armament package and fire control system proved highly successful with the standard L23 tungsten APFSDS-T projectile being highly accurate and lethal out to a range of some 3000 metres. The new L26 APFSDS kinetic energy projectile had only limited use (only 88 being fired in total during combat) whilst the L31 HESH projectile was used in over 50% of the anti-armour engagements. The L31 proved particularly useful, especially against the lighter armour targets, where the tendency was to destroy them in spectacular fashion. An Iraqi T-55 tank

Top left: Challenger 1 MBT with turret traversed to right side.   Bottom left: Challenger 1 Mk 3 during Desert Storm with camouflage netting draped over side skirt.   Top right: Side view of Challenger 1s showing the low turret shape and armour configuration.   Bottom right: Rear view of Challenger 1 showing additional fuel drums.

was also destroyed by a first round hit from a Challenger main gun, being used in the direct fire role with HESH, at the extreme range of 5100 metres.

Specification:
First prototype: 1983
First production: 1983-1990 (420 built)
Current user: UK
Crew: 4
Combat weight: 62 000 kg
Ground pressure: 0.97 kg/cm²
Length gun forwards: 11.56 m
Width (with skirts): 3.52 m
Height (without AA gun): 2.5 m
Ground clearance: 0.5 m
Max. road speed: 56 km/h
Maximum range: 400 km
Fording: unprepared 1.1 m
Gradient: 60%
Side slope: 40%
Vertical obstacle: 0.9 m
Trench: 2.8 m
Powerpack: Perkins Engines (Shrewsbury) Condor 12V 1200 liquid-cooled diesel developing 1200 hp and coupled to a David Brown Gear Industries TN37 automatic transmission
Armament: (main) 1 x 120 mm gun (64 rounds); (coaxial) 1 x 7.62 mm MG; (anti-aircraft) 1 x 7.62 mm MG; (smoke dischargers) 2 x 5

Challenger 1 showing rough terrain capability.

118

The Challenger 1 CRARRV support vehicle.

Vickers Defence Systems **Chieftain FV4201/Improved Chieftain FV4030/1 UK**

The **Chieftain** MBT was developed from 1958 onwards with the first full production standard vehicles being delivered to the British Army in 1966. These Mk 2 tanks equipped the 11th Hussars in BAOR. Over the years a number of models have been produced. These are:

Mk 2 – first full production model with 650 hp L60 engine.

Mk 3 – 1969 model with improved reliability L60 650 hp engine and running gear, new auxiliary generator and provision for laser rangefinder unit. Successive production improvements were Mk3/S and Mk3/3. The latter with

the L60 720 hp diesel engine.

Mk 3/3(P) – export version of MK 3/3 for Iran.

Mk 5 – with uprated 720 hp diesel, extended range 12.7 mm RMG, new NBC system and many internal/external equipment and stowage improvements.

Mk 5/2 (K) – export version of Mk 5 for Kuwait – 165 delivered.

Mk 5/5(P) – export version of Mk 5 for Iran – total of 707.

Mk 3/3(P) and Mk 5/5(P) delivered. Captures by Iraq of both types used by Jordan – 90 in total.

Mk 6 – upgraded Mk 2 with new

powerpack and extended range RMG.

Mk 7 – upgraded Mk 3/Mk 3S with Mk 6 modifications. 18 Mk 7/2C loaned to Oman.

Mk 8 – upgraded Mk 3/3 with Mk 6 modifications.

Mk 9 – is the Mk 6 fitted with Improved Fire Control System (IFCS).

Mk 10 – is the Mk 7 with IFCS.

Mk 11 – is the Mk 8 with IFCS, TOGS, new NBC pack and the Stillbrew passive armour package added around front of turret and hull top behind the driver.

Mk 12 – is the Mk 5 with Mk 11 improvements. At least 325 Chieftains

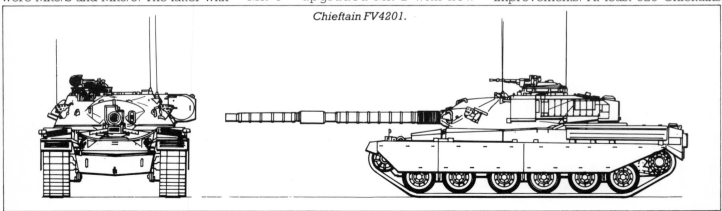

Chieftain FV4201.

120

Export version of Chieftain Mk 5 for Iranian Army.

have been fitted with TOGS.

Mk 15 – new build export version for Oman – 15 built and known locally as the Qayid-al-Ardh.

FV4030/1 – Improved Chieftain with suspension mods, greater fuel capacity and improved protection. A total of 187 built for Iran.

Under the CFE reductions numbers of Chieftain MBTs have either been sold off in a demiliterised state or reduced to scrap. A further 300 or so may be sold to Pakistan following an extensive refit programme.

Support vehicles based or built on the Chieftain chassis include the **Chieftain ARV** (**FV4204** – for Iran, Jordan (undelivered Iranian vehicles) and the UK), the **Chieftain AVLB** (**FV4205** – for the UK and Iran) and the **Chieftain AVLB Mk 6** (11 converted from Mk 1 tanks in 1984-86 for the UK), the **Chieftain MBT/bulldozer**, the **Chieftain MBT/Pearson Trackwidth Mineplough** and the **Chieftain Armoured Vehicle Royal Engineers** (**CH ARVE** – in two distinct conversion series for the UK, the first in 1986 of 12 interim vehicles and the second in 1991-94 of 48 production vehicles).

Specification:

First prototype: 1959
First production: 1963-1985 (2265 built)
Current users: Iran, Jordan, Kuwait, Oman, UK
Crew: 4
Combat weight: Mk 3 54 100 kg;
Mk 5 55 000 kg
Ground pressure: Mk 3 0.84 kg/cm^2; Mk 5 0.91 kg/cm^2
Length gun forwards: 10.8 m
Width (over skirts): 3.5 m
Height (without AA gun): 2.82 m
Ground clearance: 0.51 m
Max. road speed: 48 km/h
Maximum range: 400-500 km
Fording: unprepared 1.07 m
Gradient: 60%
Side slope: 40%
Vertical obstacle: 0.91 m
Trench: 3.15 m
Powerpack: Mk 3 – Leyland L60 diesel developing 720 hp and coupled to a SCG TN12 semi-automatic transmission;
Mk 5 – as Mk 3 but diesel engine uprated to 750 hp
Armament: (main) 1 x 120 mm gun (Mk 3 42 rounds, Mk 5 64 rounds);
(ranging) 1 x 12.7 mm MG (not in UK vehicles;
(coaxial) 1 x 12.7 mm MG (not in UK vehicles);
(anti-aircraft) 1 x 7.62 mm MG;
(smoke dischargers) 2 x 6

Opposite:
Export version of Chieftain FV4204 used by Iranian and Jordanian armies.

Vickers Defence Systems Mk 1/Mk 3 UK

Mk 1 – slightly different in appearance to the Indian Vijayanta with one road wheel on either side moved backwards to improve wheel loading and slightly reduce ground pressure. The Royal Ordnance 105 mm L7A1 rifled gun is fully stabilised and is aimed by using the 1800 metre range coaxially mounted 12.7 mm ranging machine gun. A total of 70 were delivered to Kuwait in 1970-72 but none are now believed to be in service. Most were lost in the Iraqi invasion of Kuwait that preceded the Second Gulf War.

Mk 3 – this has a new turret with a commander's cupola, provision for a white-light/infra-red searchlight, a computerised Marconi Command and Control Systems EFCS 600 fire control system, an updated fully stabilised weapon control system and a gunner's sight assembly with integral laser rangefinder module. The 105 mm gun is fitted with a thermal sleeve. The 12.7mm ranging machine gun is retained for back-up in case the primary fire control system fails.

Support vehicles produced on the Mk 3 chassis include the **Vickers Armoured Bridgelayer** and the **Vickers Armoured Repair and Recover Vehicle** (**ARRV**). The former has been bought by Nigeria (at least 12) and the latter by Kenya (7 delivered), Nigeria (at least 10 delivered) and Tanzania (2-3 delivered for use with its Chinese Type 59 MBTs).

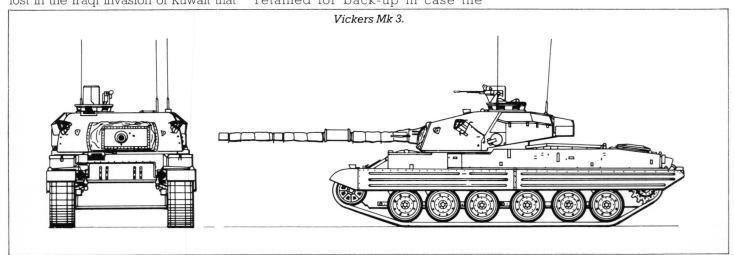

Vickers Mk 3.

Specification:

First prototype: Mk 1 1963; Mk 3 1975
First production: 1970-1972 (70 built); Mk 3 1978-current (production as required with 146 built to-date)
Current users: Mk 3 – Kenya, Nigeria, Tanzania (ARV only)
Crew: 4
Combat weight: Mk 1 38 600 kg; Mk 3 38 700 kg
Ground pressure: 0.87 kg/cm^2
Length gun forwards: Mk 1 9.73 m; Mk 3 9.78 m
Width: 3.2 m
Height (without AA gun): Mk 1 2.44 m; Mk 3 2.47 m
Ground clearance: Mk 1 0.41 m; Mk 2 2.47 m
Max. road speed: Mk 1 48 km/h; Mk 3 50 km/h
Maximum range: Mk 1 480 km; Mk 3 530 km
Fording: unprepared 1.14 m
Gradient: 60%
Side slope: 30%
Vertical obstacle: Mk 1 0.9 m; Mk 3 0.8 m
Powerpack: Mk 1 – Leyland L60 Mk 4B liquid-cooled diesel developing 650 hp and coupled to an SCG TN12 series transmission; Mk 3 – Detroit Diesel 12V-71T V-12 air-cooled turbocharged diesel developing 725 hp and coupled to an SCG TN12 series transmission

Armament: (main) 1 x 105 mm gun (Mk 1 44 rounds, Mk 3 50 rounds); (coaxial) 1 x 12.7 mm MG; (anti-aircraft) 1 x 7.62 mm MG; (smoke dischargers) 2 x 6

Vickers Defence Systems Mk 3 MBT.

Centurion

Danish Centurion – approximately 110 basic Centurion Mk 3 upgraded to Mk 5 standard retaining 20 pdr gun and 105 other Mk 3 converted to Centurion Mk 5/2 standard with a 105 mm L7A3 rifled gun firing APFSDS-T, smoke, HESH and APDS ammunition types, an Ericsson laser rangefinder sight for the gunner and a 12.7 mm MG anti-aircraft gun.

Mk 7 – fitted with the 20 pdr gun (with 63 rounds of ammunition), extra fuel tankage, upgraded weapon control system and many other minor improvements to internal/external features and equipment. The Mk 7/2 is the Mk 7 upgunned with the 105 mm L7 rifled gun.

Mk 8/1 – uparmoured version of the Mk 8 with additional frontal glacis plate armour patch. The main gun remained the 20 pdr with 63 rounds of main gun ammunition.

Swedish Centurion Strv 101 – approx 170 Mk 10 delivered in 1960 and subsequently upgunned with 105 mm L7 rifled guns and 8 mm MGs, fitted with turret direction indicator, American radios and new auxiliary engine.

Swedish Centurion Strv 102 – approx 270 Mk 3/Mk 5 delivered early to mid fifties (as the Strv 81) with most upgraded to Strv 102 standard with over 110 minor changes made and fitting of 105 mm gun.

Swedish Centurion Strv 104 – in the early eighties the Strv 101 and 102 started further modernisation pro-

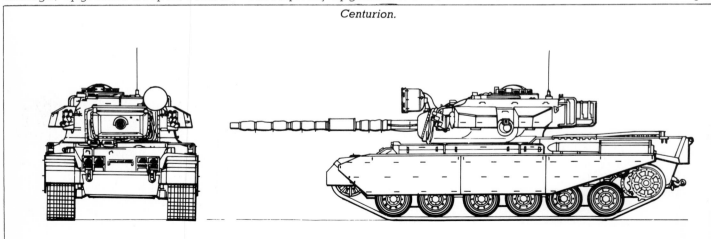

Centurion.

Swedish Army Strv-101 Centurion.

grammes involving the fitting of an Ericsson gunner's laser rangefinder sight, a Bofors integrated Tank Fire Control system, the 71 mm Lyran illuminating twin launcher system and an AVDS-1790-2DC 750 hp V-12 air-cooled diesel engine coupled to an Allison CD-850-6A automatic transmission. By the early nineties over half the Strv 101/102 fleet had been modernised to what is believed to be known as the Strv 104 standard.

Tariq – 293 Jordanian Centurions of various marks were converted during 1981-85 to a single standard. This involved the fitting of a 105 mm M68 rifled gun, a Belgian SABCA Atlas Mk 1 computerised fire control system with integral gunner's laser rangefinder sight assembly module. a 750 hp TCM AVDS-1790-2CC turbo-charged diesel powerpack with automatic transmission, hydro-pneumatic suspension and Cadillac Gage Textron turret power control and weapon/turret stabilisation systems.

Combat support vehicles still in service based on the Centurion chassis include the **Mk 2 ARV** (**FV4006**), the **Centurion BARV** (**FV4018**), the **Centurion 165 AVRE** (**FV4003**) and the **Centurion 105 AVRE** (the last three vehicles are only used by the British Army).

The Mk 5 AVRE saw combat service in the Second Gulf War as the main combat engineers break-through vehicle for Iraq border fortifications. It was fitted with additional add-on passive and ERA packages and used with the Track Width mine plough system. Both the 105 AVRE and 165 AVRE are being replaced by the Chieftain AVRE.

Specification:
First prototype: Mk 1 1945
First production: 1946-62 (4422 built of Mark numbers 1/2/3/5//7//8/9/1- – the Mark numbers 6/11/12/13 were conversions of earlier models)
Current users: Denmark (Mk 5, Mk 5/2), Jordan (Tariq conversion), Singapore (Mk 5/Mk 7) Somalia (Mk 8/1), Sweden (Strv 101 – Mk 10 equivalent and Strv 102 – Mk 33/5 upgrades)
Crew: 4
Combat weight: 50 730 kg
Ground pressure: 0.9 kg/cm^2
Length gun forwards: Mk 5 9.56 m; Mk 5/2 9.85 m
Width (with skirts): 3.39 m
Height (without AA gun): 2.94 m
Ground clearance: 0.46 m
Max. road speed: 35 km/h
Maximum range: 100 km
Fording: unprepared 1.45 m
Gradient: 60%
Side slope: 30%
Vertical obstacle: 0.91 m
Trench: 3.35mm
Powerpack: Rolls Royce Mk IVB V-12 liquid cooled petrol engine developed 650 hp and coupled to a Merrit-Brown Z51R manual transmission
Armament: (main) Mk 5 – 1 x 20 pdr gun (65 rounds), Mk 5/2 – 1 x 105 mm gun 64 rounds); (coaxial) 1 x 7.62 mm MG; (anti-aircraft) 1 x 7.62 mm MG; (smoke dischargers) 2 x 6

Opposite: British Army Centurion 165 AVRE with additional armour passing a knocked out Iraqi T-62 during the Second Gulf War; it later demolished the ediface on the right of the picture.

129

General Dynamics
Abrams M1A1/M1A1(HA)/M1A2   USA

The General Dynamics, Land Systems Division **M1A1 Abrams** is the evolutionary successor to the M1/ Improved M1 MBT models. Although it uses the same basic design of the Improved M1 it has a 120 mm M256 Rheinmentall smoothbore gun, collective NBC system, improved digital computer fire control system with a state-of-the-art stabilised gunner's day/night sight assembly and integral laser rangefinding/thermal imaging capabilities, improved transmission and suspension systems.

The gun fires APFSDS-T (depleted uranium type) and HEAT-MP-T ammunition. The former round is limited to US Army use only so the Egyptian Army is procuring an American built KE-T round in lieu, which is based on a Tungsten metal penetrator.

In late 1989 the US Army adopted the **M1A1 Heavy Armour** (**M1A1(HA)**) version for deployment in Europe. This has additional steel encased depleted uranium armour mesh added to the M1 standard advanced 'Chobham' type armour configuration.

In late 1990 the **M1A1 (Common Tank)** version entered production with

67 engineering changes that make the vehicle suitable for use by the US Marine Corps. It has tie-down points, fording kit attachments and the Heavy Armour package. A total of 221 were built for the US Marine Corps between 1990-92.

The follow-on **M1A2** (or M1 Block II) entered US Army field trial testing in mid-1992. This has further special passive armour hull and turret improvements to defeat kinetic and chemical energy rounds, added roof protection to reduce the threat from fielded top-attack ATGW and anti-tank bomblets, a

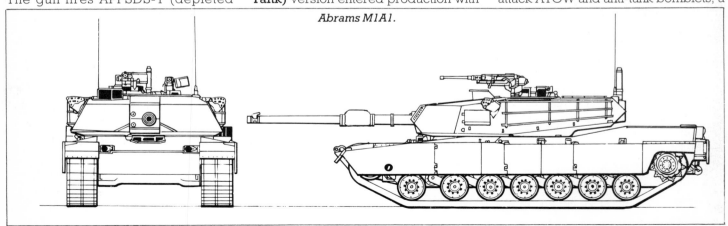

Abrams M1A1.

Abrams M1A2 firing at night target during second Gulf War.

complete digital Intervehicular Information System (IVIS) to replace the current wiring, independent Commander and Driver thermal viewing systems (the CITV and DTV systems), a POS/NAV land navigation system, an updated digital fire control system with new ballistic computer and the capability to carry and fire a new generation of advanced 120 mm 'smart' ammunition types that are currently being developed to deal with various battlefield targets.

Although only 77 new build M1A2 have been ordered for the US Army a number of older M1/M1A1 tanks are to be upgraded to varying M1A2 standards. The exact numbers have yet to be finalised although will be over 1000 in total. The programme is likely to run from 1996 onwards if funds permit.

In 1988 Egypt ordered 524 M1A1 with the majority being built under license from kit form. In addition Saudi Arabia has ordered 465 M1A2, with first deliveries due in 1994. The Saudi Arabians also have another 235 on option. Kuwait has also chosen the M1A2 as its next MBT, ordering 218 in October 1992.

During the Gulf War the M1A1 models undertook the brunt of the US Army armour battles destroying large numbers of Iraqi tanks at battle ranges of up to 3500 metres or more. The thermal viewing equipment could see targets at over 5000 metres and positively identify them at over 1000-1500 metres. They also allowed enemy positions and vehicles to be seen in the worst of the battlefield conditions, namely the thick oil-fire smoke from the burning Kuwaiti oilfields.

It was found that the 120 mm M829A1 APFSDS-T rounds used could be fired through five foot thick sand berms used to protect Iraqi tanks in hull down positions and still destroy the target. In another instance an M1A1 hit the turret of a T-72 with an anti-tank round which passed straight through the turret's side armour, the turret interior and the armour on the other side of the turret and then went on to hit and destroy a second T-72. On another occasion an M1A1 destroyed a T-72 by penetrating its frontal armour at a range of 3500 metres.

The M1A1 surviveability proved to be on a par with the Israeli Merkava: none were totally destroyed, nine were permanently disabled (mostly by friendly action or in two cases by their own crews when the vehicles had to be abandoned) and nine damaged (mainly by mines) but were considered repairable. Only a few dozen crewmen were injured in combat.

At least seven M1A1s were hit by 125 mm fire from T-72, non had any serious damage caused. One M1A1 suffered two direct hits from anti-tank sabot rounds fired from a T-72 at approximately 500 metres away which simply bounced off its armour.

The main danger faced by the Abrams was the myriads of Iraqi anti-tank mines obtained from both Eastern and Western sources and these weapons caused the disablement of several M1A1s.

The US Marine Corps also used 60 M1A1(HA) and 18 M1A1 Common Tanks in the Gulf War, but had to borrow the former from the US Army. These equipped the 2nd Marine Tank Battalion and the 4th Marine Tank Battalion assigned to units of the 1st Marine Expeditionary Force.

Opposite: Abrams M1A2 on road trials.

US Army Abrams M1A1.

Specification:

First prototype: M1A1 1981; M1A2 1990

First production: M1A1 – 1985-current (2500 built plus 25 for Egypt in 1991 and further 499 in kit form for construction at local factory over period 1992-98); M1A1(HA) – 1988-1993 (2302 built); M1A2 – 1992-current (77 built 1992-93 for US Army, batches of 315 and 150 for Saudi Arabian Army from 1993-96 with option on further 235, plus additional 236 for Kuwait)

Current users: M1A1 – Egypt, USA (US Army and US Marine Corps); M1A1(HA) – US Army; M1A1-US Army, (on order for Kuwait and Saudi Arabia)

Crew: 4

Combat weight: M1A1 57 155 kg; M1A1(HA) 63 738 kg; M1A2 61 690 kg

Ground pressure: n/av

Length gun forwards: 9.83 m

Width : 3.66 m

Height (without AA gun): 2.44 m

Ground clearance: 0.43 m

Max. road speed: 55 km/h

Maximum range: 460 km

Fording: unprepared 1.22 m

Gradient: 60%

Side slope: 40%

Vertical obstacle: 1.24 m

Trench: 2.74 m

Powerpack: Textron Lycoming AGT 1500 multi-fuel gas turbine developing 1500 hp and coupled to an X-1100-3B automatic transmission

Armament: (main) 1 x 120 mm gun (40 rounds); (coaxial) 1 x 7.62 mm MG; (anti-aircraft) 1 x 12.7 mm and 1 x 7.62 mm MG; (smoke dischargers) 2 x 6

Abrams M1A1 at speed in desert conditions.

General Dynamics Basic **Abrams M1/**
Improved Performance M1

USA

The **Basic M1 Abrams** was developed in the seventies by General Dynamics, Land Systems Division as the follow-on to the M60 MBT series with considerably improved protection, firepower, mobility and maintenance aspects.

The major new feature, however, was the fitting of a multi-fuel gas turbine engine. The armament is the standard 105 mm M68 series rifled gun with a full solution CDC M1 digital computer fire control system coupled to a sophisticated gunner's day/night sight. The gun can fire APFSDS-T, APDS-T, APERS-T, HEAT-T, HEP-T and smoke round ammunition types. The armour is essentially an American improved version of the British Chobham special armour package, and is the reason for the box-like appearance of the Abrams.

The **Improved Performance M1 (IPM1)** is basically the same as the M1 but with key modifications to take advantages of features that are included in the follow-on M1A1 programme. These include an uprated suspension system to enhance its cross-country combat performance, various transmission improvements, modified final drive, an enhanced armour package and the addition of a turret bustle basket. Two battalions of these IPM1 tanks were assigned to the US Army units in South Korea.

An add-on package to convert M1 family vehicles into a bulldozer tank is used by the US Army. The Israeli Track Width Mine Plough (TWMP) has also been procured for use with the M1 series under the designation Mine Clearing Blade System (MCBS).

An adaptor kit is also used to fit the General Dynamics Land Systems Division mine roller kit. In conjunction

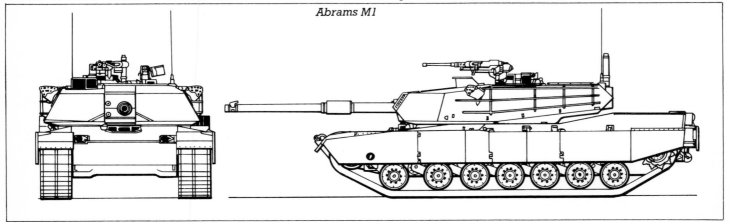

Abrams M1

M1 Abrams with 105mm main gun of US Army's Third Armoured Division during mid-eighties exercises in Germany.

with the roller the M1 vehicle also carries a Vehicle Magnetic Signature Duplicator (VEMASID) unit which projects a magnetic signature ahead of the tank in order to explode magnetically fused mines which are not swept effectively by the rollers action.

In the late eighties a development contract was placed with BMY and TAAS – Israel Industries to develop a 26 metre Heavy Assault Bridge (HAB) system with Class 70 load classifications for use by the M1 fleet. The bridge is to be carried and launched from a variant of the M1 MBT chassis.

Another development contract was placed with General Dynamics Land Systems Division and MAN of Germany to produce a three-part 26 m HAB version of the latter company's Leguan bridge system. A third HAB contract was placed with Southwest Mobile Systems and Thomson Defence Products of the UK, using the latter's 26 m Thomson Modular Bridge No 10 design of the UK MoD's 'Bridging for the Nineties' programme as its basis. The three designs are undergoing final evaluation with a total of 106 M1 HAB of the winning design required from FY97 onwards.

A private venture prototype of a ARV variant known as the **Abrams** Recovery Vehicle was also developed in the late eighties by General Dynamics Land Systems Division, with the capability to carry, change and fit a complete Abrams gas turbine powerpack unit in the field. Based on the M1A1 chassis this vehicle has not been ordered by the US Army.

Approximately 580 or so M1 and IPM1 Abrams were deployed to the Gulf region in the initial stages of Desert Shield, primarily with the 24th Infantry Division (Mechanized) and the 1st Cavalry Division. They where subsequently replaced in these units by M1A1s transferred from European storage sites. The M1A1 fleet eventually totalled some 2300 US Army vehicles (1178 M1A1 and 594 M1A1(HA) in operational units with another 528 M1A1 in operationally ready float status and theatre war reserve stocks) plus 16 M1A1 and 60 M1A1(HA) US Marine Corps vehicles in the 2nd and 4th Marine Tank battalions.

Specification:
First prototype: M1 1976; Improved Product M1 1984
First production: M1 1980-1985 (2374 built); Improved Product M1 1984-1986 (894 built)
Current user: USA
Crew: 4
Combat weight: M1 54 550 kg; IPM1 55 550 kg
Ground pressure: 0.96 kg/cm^2
Length gun forwards: 9.77 m
Width: 3.65 m
Height (without AA gun): 2.38 m
Ground clearance: 0.43 m
Max. road speed: 72.5 km/h
Maximum range: 500 km
Fording: unprepared 1.22 m
Gradient: 60%
Side slope: 40%
Vertical obstacle: 1.24 m
Trench: 2.74 m
Powerpack: Textron Lycoming AGT 1500 multi-fuel gas turbine developing 1500 hp and coupled to an X-1100-3B automatic transmission
Armament: (main) 1 x 105 mm gun (55 rounds); (coaxial) 1 x 7.62 mm MG; (anti-aircraft) 1 x 12.7 mm and 1 x 7.62 mm MG; (smoke dischargers) 2 x 6

M1 Abrams on US Army tank transporter.

M60A3/M60A3 TTS Patton USA

The **M60A3 Patton** followed the M60A1 version into production and introduced a number of significant improvements. These include the fitting of a fully stabilised 105 mm M68 rifled gun with thermal sleeve, gunner's laser rangefinder unit, passive night vision equipment, more reliable powerpack, running gear components and tracks and the M21 ballistic computer fire control system.

The latter is considerably enhanced by the conversion of the basic M60A3 to the **M60A3 TTS** configuration. This involves the fitting of a Texas Instruments AN/VGS-2 Tank Thermal Sight (TTS) as a replacement for the existing gunner's M35E1 day/night (image intensifier) vision periscope. Incorpor-

ated into the AN/VSG-2 is a laser rangefinder unit. Over 5000 US Army M60A3s have been produced/ converted to the M60A3 TTS standard together with 250 Saudi Arabian M60A3 (as new build procurement/ M60A1 conversions). Saudi Arabia used its M60A3 tanks during Operation Desert Storm.

The ammunition types carried can include APDS-T, APERS-T, HEAT-T, APFSDS-T, HEP-T and smoke types.

Taiwan has also produced a hybrid MBT design, the M48H Brave Tiger, which mates the M60A3 chassis and powerplant with a modernised M48 turret fitted with a locally produced 105mm rifled gun, advanced digital computer fire control system and laser

rangefinder with a thermal imaging sight assembly. A total of 450 M48H MBTs were completed by mid-1993. The Taiwanese army also use 150 M60A3 and the Taiwanese Marine Corps 110 M60A3 TTS.

As part of the CFE reductions approximately 2000 M60 series tanks have become surplus to US requirements and these are being cascaded to minimal cost to both NATO and approved American client states.

The only support vehicles based on M60 chassis are the M60A1/M60A3 MBT fitted with a mine roller system, the M60 MBT series with M9 bulldozer kit, the **M60 AVLB** with scissors bridge (for the US Army, Israel, Singapore and Spain).

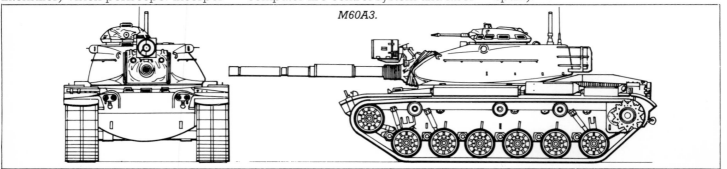
M60A3.

US Army M60A3.

The M60 series can also be used to push the 122 metre long M3A1 and the 90 odd metre long M157 rigid assembly projected HE mine-clearing charges into enemy minefields.

Specification:
First prototype: M60A3 1978
First production: M60A3 1978-1990 (new build plus conversions of M60A1)
Current users: M60A3 – Austria, Bahrain, Egypt, Jordan, Sudan, Taiwan, Tunisia, USA; M60A3 TTS – Saudi Arabia, Spain, Taiwan (Marine Corps), USA

Crew: 4
Combat weight: 52 620 kg
Ground pressure: 0.87 kg/cm²
Length gun forwards: 9.44 m
Width: 3.63 m
Height (with AA gun and cupola): 3.27 m
Ground clearance: 0.45 m
Max. road speed: 48 km/h
Maximum range: 480 km
Fording: unprepared 1.22 m
Gradient: 60%

Side slope: 30%
Vertical obstacle: 0.91 m
Trench: 2.6 m
Powerpack: AVDS-1790-2C RISE V-12 air-cooled diesel developing 750 hp coupled to an Allison CD-850-6A automatic transmission
Armament: (main) 1 x 105 mm gun (63 rounds); (coaxial) 1 x 7.62 mm MG; (anti-aircraft) 1 x 12.7 mm MG; (smoke dischargers) 2 x 6

US Army M60A3 showing uncovered six-round British smoke dischargers on turret side.

US Army M60A3 with thermal sleeve on 105 mm rifled gun.

M60/M60A1 Patton USA

The **XM60** 105 mm gun tank proto- types were an outgrowth of the M48 series with the **M60** production model being equipped with the old hemi- spherical M48-style turret and a new design of hull chassis. These were quickly followed by the definitive **M60A1** model which used a narrower shaped turret with greater ballistic protection and many internal/external equipment and stowage arrangement changes.

The main armament is the 105 mm M68 series rifled gun with bore evacuator. An NBC system is fitted and a complete set of night fighting vision equipment is carried including M35E1/ M36E1 passive day/night comman- der's and gunner's sight assemblies, an AN/VSS-1 or AN/VSS-3A white light/infra-red searchlight unit over the gun mantlet and an AN/VVS-2 driver's night vision periscope viewer.

In addition to the main production models a total of 526 **M60A2** tanks, combat weight 51 980 kg, were built from 1966 onwards. Armed with a 152 mm M162 gun/Shillelagh missile launcher and 46 HE-T/HEAT-T-MP/ canister/smoke rounds/missiles they proved troublesome in service and were withdrawn from use for con- version to support vehicles.

Egypt and the US Marine Corps used M60A1s during Operation Desert Storm. The former fitted their vehicles with a 1700 kg explosive reactive armour (ERA) package for use in the Gulf. All Marine Corps M60A1s have

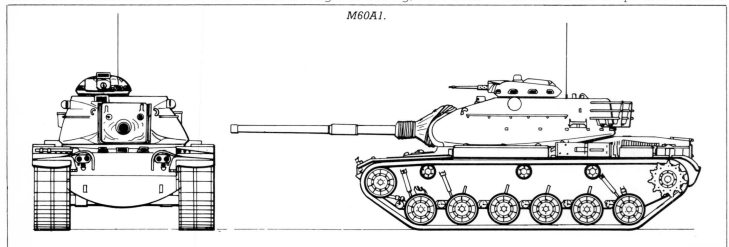

M60A1.

M60A1 of the US Army.

now been withdrawn from service. Ten ex-Marine Corps M60A1 (ERA) have been given to the Italian Army for use in Somalia, as the have lost at least two of their own M60A1s to light anti-armour weapons.

Apart from the M60 support vehicles mentioned in the M60A3 entry there is also the **M728 Combat Engineer Vehicle (CEV)** built using M60A1 design features. This 53 200 kg four-man crew vehicle is armed with a 165 mm M135 demolition gun and fitted with bulldozer blade and 'A'-frame. It is used by the US, Israeli, Saudi Arabian and Singaporean armies.

Specification:
First prototype: 1958
First production: M60 – 1960-1962 (2205 built); M60A1 – 1962-1980 (7753 built)
Current users: M60 – USA; M60A1 – Egypt, Greece, Iran, Italy (including 200 licensed-built in late sixties), Jordan, Oman, Spain (to be locally upgraded to M60A3), Thailand, USA, Republic of Yemen
Crew: 4
Combat weight: M60 49 710 kg; M60A1 52 610 kg (54 310 kg with ERA)
Ground pressure: M60 .8 kg/cm²; M60A1 0.87 kg/cm²
Length gun forwards: M60 9.31 m; M60A1 9.44m

Width: 3.63 m
Height (with AA gun and cupola): M60 3.21 m; M60A1 3.27 m
Ground clearance: 0.46 m
Max. road speed: 48 km/h
Maximum range: 500 km
Fording: unprepared 1.22 m
Gradient: 60%
Side slope: 30%
Vertical obstacle: 0.91 m
Trench: 2.6 m

Powerpack: AVDS-1790-2A V-12 air-cooled diesel developing 750 hp and coupled to an Allison CD-850-6 (M60) or CD-850-6A (M60A1) automatic transmission
Armament: (main) 1 x 105 mm gun (M60 57 rounds, M60A1 63 rounds); (coaxial) 1 x 7.62 mm MG; (anti-aircraft) 1 x 12.7 mm MG; (smoke dischargers) 2 x 6 (M60A1 only)

M60 Series MBT used in mine warfare disposal/detecting programme.

M60 series MBT with Track Width Mine Plough Unit fitted.

M48A5 Patton USA

The **M48A5** conversion programme was initially started to bring the M48 series tanks in the US Army up to an equivalent M60A1 standard. The first vehicles chosen were 360 M48A3s as these were deemed the easiest model to convert. In the hull a new top loading M60 style air cleaner was fitted with a solid state regulator, the ammunition stowage was modified to accept 54 105 mm rounds, the suspension and tracks were upgraded, the engine and transmission changed, a 105 mm M68 rifled gun installed and a turret basked added. An Israeli model low profile

commander's cupola was also fitted. Other countries also pursued their own conversion programmes, these include:

South Korea – over 700 of the 1100 or so M48, M48A1, M48A2C and M48A3 Pattons supplied to the country have been completely rebuilt to the **M48A5K** standard by Hyundai. The tank is fitted with a license built 105 mm M68 main gun, modern fire control system, new powerpack and modified suspension. The M48A5K is considered to be more capable than either the M48A5 or M60A1 MBTs.

Spain – During the late seventies 165 M48/M48A1 and M48A2 Pattons were modified to **M48A5E** standard by utilizing American supplied M48A5 upgrade kits. These were further upgraded during 1983-85 with full solution digital fire control systems, integral laser rangefinder module and improved gunner day/night sight assembly. The designation changed to **M48A5E1**.

Taiwan – Some 550 M48A1/M48A2/ M48A3 are being locally modified to the M48A5 standard using conversion kits. Apart from the 105 mm rifled gun

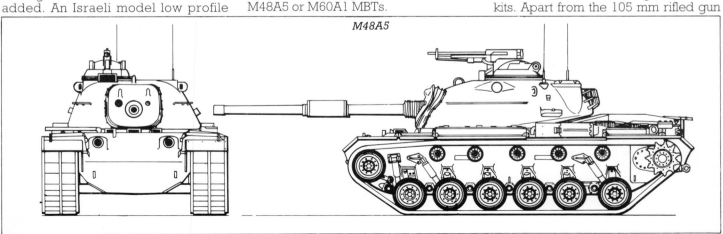

M48A5

and new powerplant the conversions includes the installation of a laser rangefinder and modern digital computer fire control system.

Turkey – some 2783 M48 series Pattons were delivered to Turkey between 1950 and 1981. Most have now undergone rebuilding at two US sponsored conversion plants built in 1982-84 to one of the following configurations:

M48A5T1 – some 1200 plus conversion of early model M48 series tanks to the M48A5 configuration. Apart from receiving a locally-built 105 mm L7 series main gun a full active/passive night fighting capability has been fitted. Subsequent modification adds a main armament stabilisation system.

M48A5T2 – some 900 plus conversions to a more advanced level that the M48A5T1. The additional improvements include a ballistic computer fire control system and an AN/VSG-2 Tank Thermal Sight for the gunner.

The US Army conversion of the M48A1/M48A2/M48A2C was a more involved and costlier operation as nearly 300 hull and 20 turret modifications were needed to bring it to the same M48A5 standard.

Support vehicles based on the M48 chassis included the **M67 series flamethrower tank** (none left in service) and the **M48 AVLB** with scissors bridge (used by Israel and Taiwan).

The M48 automotive components were also used as the basis for the M88 ARV series with over 2200 produced. A number of other AFV's also use automotive components of the M48 series.

No M48A5 series MBTs remain in US Army regular or reserve unit service, all have been withdrawn for storage and subsequent scrapping or use as military aid.

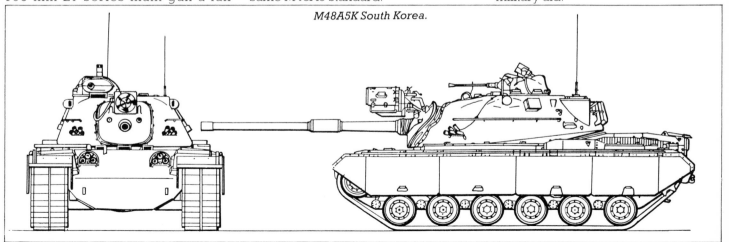

M48A5K South Korea.

Specification:
First prototype: 1975
First production: 1975-1979 (conversion programme of M48A1/M48A2/M48A2C/M48A3 vehicles)
Current users: Greece, Iran, Jordan, South Korea, Lebanon, Morocco, Norway, Pakistan, Portugal, Spain, Taiwan, Thailand, Tunisia, Turkey
Crew: 4
Combat weight: 49 090 kg
Ground pressure: 0.88 kg/cm^2
Length gun forwards: 9.47 m
Width: 3.63 m
Height (with cupola): 3.29 m
Ground clearance: 0.41 m
Max. road speed: 48 km/h
Maximum range: 500 km
Fording: unprepared 1.22 m
Gradient: 60%
Side slope: 40%
Vertical obstacle: 0.9 m
Trench: 2.6 m
Powerpack: M48A1/M48A2/M48A2C conversion – AV1790-2D RISE V-12 air-cooled diesel developing 750 hp and coupled to an Allison CD-850-6A automatic transmission; M48A3 conversion – as M48A1 but with an AVDS-1790-2A RISE model diesel
Armament: (main) 1 x 105 mm gun (54 rounds); (coaxial) 1 x 7.62 mm MG; (anti-aircraft) 1 x 12.7 mm and 1 x 7.62 mm or 2 x 7.62 mm MG; (smoke dischargers) 2 x 6

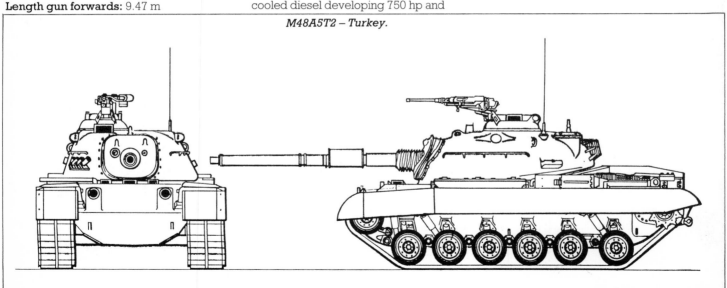

M48A5T2 – Turkey.

M48A5 as used by US Army, note IR/white light searchlight over 105mm main gun.

M48A1/M48A2/M48A3 Series Patton   USA

M48 – first production model with none believed to be remaining in service. The M48C was a training version with mild steel hull. A number were converted to M48A2C standard.

M48A1 – 1800 built but never received a T-series development designation. Fitted with fully enclosed commander's cupola and new suspension/running gear components.

M48A2 – also known as Product Improved M48 with redesigned engine compartment to incorporate new fuel injection petrol engine, increased fuel load and to reduce the battlefield IR signature. The running gear was changed and the 90 mm main gun control systems and the tanks fire control system with its gunner's stereoscopic rangefinder sight updated. The **M48A2C** production variant had its fire control system graduated in metres rather than yards and switched over to a coincidence type gunner's sight.

M48A3 – a rebuild of the earlier M48A1/M48A2 models with the petrol engine replaced by the diesel engine and transmission of the M60A1, a collective NBC system fitted and further improvements to the fire control system, commander's cupola, transmission and running gear.

A number of other countries also undertook conversion programmes. These included:

Germany – a total of 650 M48A2 Pattons were rebuilt by Wegmann during 1978 – 80 to the **M48A2GA2** standard. The 90 mm gun was replaced by a 105 mm L7 series rifled gun fitted with a thermal sleeve, 46 rounds of 105 mm ammunition were carried as the basic load and a full night fighting capability was added together with a passive Low Light Level Television (LLLTV) aiming and observation camera system over the gun mantlet. Under CFE these vehicles will either be destroyed or cascaded to suitable friendly countries.

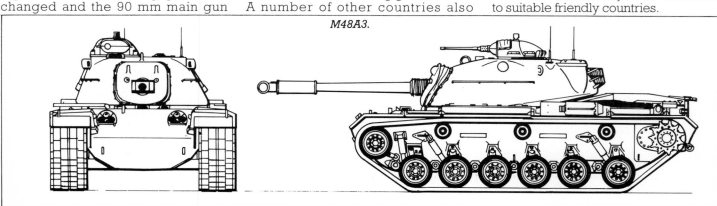

M48A3.

Spain – In the late seventies the Spanish Marines took delivery of 19 locally modified **M48A3E** Patton tanks. This had a number of major modifications but retained the 90 mm main gun armament with 62 rounds.

Turkey – A total of 174 rebuilds of early model M48 pattons were undertaken initially by Wegmann of Germany and then via kit form in Turkey. based on the M48A2GA2 design the programme involved the fitting of a new engine and transmission, a locally built 105 mm L7 series rifled gun with thermal sleeve and extensive changes to the chassis, turret systems and suspension. A total of 46 105 mm rounds are carried. The

Turkish designation for these tanks is **M48T1**.

The support tank variants are dealt with in the M48A5 entry.

Specification:
First prototype: M48 1951
First production: M48A1 1955-1956; M48A2 1956-1959 (total of 11 703 M48/M48A1/M48A2 vehicles built)
Current users: M48A1 – Greece, South Korea, Taiwan, Turkey; M48A2 – Greece, Norway, Turkey; M48A3 – Greece, South Korea, Morocco, Spain, Tunisia
Crew: 4
Combat weight: M48A1/A3 47 273 kg; M48A2 47 727 kg

Ground pressure: 0.83 kg/cm²
Length gun forwards: M48A1 8.73m; M48A2/A3 8.69 m
Width: M48A1/A2/A3 3.63 m
Height (without AA gun): M48A1 3.13 m; M48A2 3.09 m; M48A3 3.12 m
Ground clearance: M48A1 0.38 m; M48A2 0.42 m; M48A3 0.41 m
Max. road speed: M48A1 42 km/h;M48A2/A3 48 km/h
Maximum range: M48A1* 216 km; M48A2* 400 km; M48A3 496 km/h
*with jettisonable external fuel tanks
Fording: unprepared 1.22 m
Gradient: 60%
Side slope: 30%
Vertical obstacle: 0.91 m

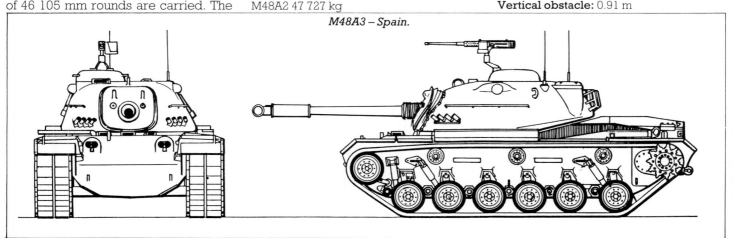

M48A3 – Spain.

Trench: 2.6 m

Powerpack: M48A1 – AV1790-7C V-12 air-cooled petrol engine developing 810 hp and coupled to an Allison CD-850-4B transmission; M48A2 – as M48A1 but AVI 1790-8 825 hp engine and CD-850-5 transmission; M48A3 – as M48 but AVDS-1790-2A 750 hp diesel engine and CD-850-6 transmission

Armament: (main) 1 x 90 mm gun (M48A1 60 rounds, M48A2 64 rounds, M48A3 62 rounds); (coaxial) 1 x 7.62 mm MG; (anti-aircraft) 1 x 12.7 mm MG

Right: US Army M48A2, almost all US Army early M48 Patton variants were rebuilt to the later M48A5 standard.

M47/M47M Patton   USA

The **M47** entered production during the Korean War period and was basically a T42 turret fitted on a new hull. The vehicle apparently never entered a T-series prototype stage.

The 90 mm gun fitted is the M36 model with the gunner using a basic stereoscopic rangefinder sight. If the bow machine gun is retained then the basic ammunition load is 71 rounds, if it is removed then the load can be increased to a maximum 105 rounds. The ammunition types fired include APC-T, APERS-T, AP-T, HE-T, HEAT-FS, HVAP-T, APFSDS-T, canister and smoke. No NBC system is fitted.

The **M47M** is a BMY designed upgrade that incorporated the fitting of the running gear, engine, transmission and electrohydraulic turret/weapon control systems of the M60A1 MBT with numerous minor turret internal/external equipment and stowage changes. Iran built a tank plant between 1970-72 to convert 400 of its M47 Pattons and 147 Pakistani Army vehicles to this configuration.

The plant subsequently took on M48A5 conversion work and M60A1 refurbishment work for the Iranian Army and a 145 M48A1 vehicle modernisation to M48A5 package for Pakistan. Pakistan has also prototyped its own **M47M AVLB support vehicle** and may well produce small numbers for its army.

South Korea has also modified its 550 plus **M47 Patton** fleet with improved running gear and the provision of full active/passive night fighting capabilities. It has also converted other **M47s** into a simple ARV variant with a winch in place of the turret and an A-frame to lift heavy components.

During the mid seventies Spain converted 376 M47s into 330 **M47E1** and 46 **M47E2** variants. The latter having a 105 mm Rheinmetall Rh-105-30 rifled gun fitted with ammunition stowage for 44 105 mm rounds. Most of these will be phased out as surplus

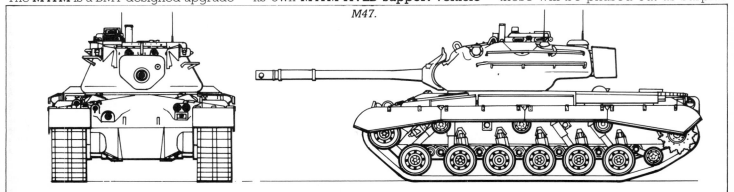

M47.

M60A1/M60A3 Pattons are received. A number of Support tank version shave also been designed by the Spanish firm Talbot SA which converted the **M47s**. These include an engineer tank, ARV and AVLB, with Spain requiring all three types.

Specification:

First prototype: M47 none; M47M 1969
First production: M47 1950-1953 (8576 built); M47M 1973-75 (547 conversions)
Current users: M47 – Greece, Italy, South Korea, Portugal, Somalia, Turkey M47M – Iran, Pakistan
Crew: M47 – 5; M47M – 4
Combat weight: M47 46 170 kg; M47M 46 810 kg

Ground pressure: 0.94 kg/cm²
Length gun forwards: M47 8.51 m; M47M 8.55 m
Width: 3.38 m
Height (without AA gun): 3.02 m
Ground clearance: 0.47 m
Max. road speed: M47 48 km/h; M47M 55 km/h
Maximum range: M47 130 km;M47M 600 km
Fording: unprepared 1.22 m
Gradient: 60%
Side slope: 30%
Vertical obstacle: 0.91 m
Trench: 2.6 m
Powerpack: M47 – AV1790-5B, -7 or -7 V-12 air-cooled petrol engine developing 810 hp and coupled to an Allison CD-850-4, -4A or -4B transmission; M47M – AV-1790-

2A V-12 air-cooled diesel developing 750 hp and coupled to an Allison CD-850-6A transmission
Armament: (main) 1 x 90 mm gun (M47 71 rounds, M47M 79 rounds); (bow) 1 x 7.62 mm MG (removed in M47M); (coaxial) 1 x 7.62 mm or 12.7 mm MG; (anti-aircraft) 1 x 12.7 mm MG

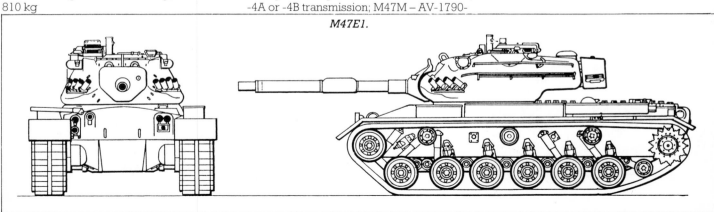

M47E1.

A ROK M47 on amphibious assault manoeuvres in South Korea.

In the late seventies Yugoslavia decided to license manufacture an indigenous MBT based on the Soviet T-72 design. Known as the **M-84** it is essentially similar with the same fully stabilised main 125 mm 2A46 smoothbore gun/22-round carrousel type autoloader arrangement and a locally designed SUV-84 fire control system. The latter resulted in the replacement of both the gunner's TPN-1-49 and commander's TKN-3 original Soviet model sights and deletion of the separate TPD-2-49 laser rangefinder and its port on the front left side of the turret.

The TPD-2-49 being no longer required as the locally developed and produced gunner's sight, the DNNS-2, has its own integral laser rangefinder module. Both this sight and the replacement commander's sight, the DKNS-2, also have passive night vision image intensifier channels.

These facilities together with a pylon mounted meteorological sensor unit on the centre-front of the turret and a ballistic computer allow the M-84 to effectively acquire, track and engage targets between 200-4000 metres in both day and night conditions using full solution fire control computations with APFSDS and HE-FRAG rounds. With HEAT-FS ammunition the maximum effective engagement range is increased to 6000 metres.

Beneath the vehicle front is the dozer blade device for digging itself into a firing position whilst attachments are available for KMT type mine-clearing equipment.

The latest version built is the **M-84A**, which has a 1000 hp diesel engine and a number of internal improvements. Command tank (with additional communications equipment) and ARV versions have also been produced.

Kuwait ordered 170 M-84, 15 **M-84 ARV** and 15 **M-84 command tanks** in mid-1989 as replacements for elderly British equipment but supplies were interrupted because of the Iraqi invasion. Approximately 80 were subsequently delivered to the Kuwaiti Army in Saudi Arabia to reequip an Armoured unit and were used during the 1991 Gulf War.

The **M-84** has also seen extensive combat use in the various internal wars within Yugoslavia: namely the Slov-

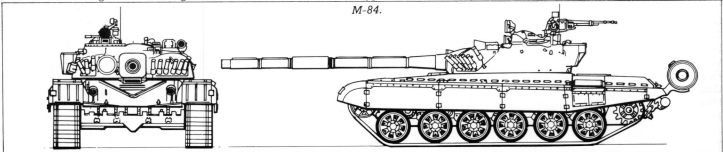

M-84.

enian, Croatian and Bosnian-Herze-govian theatres of operation. Used mainly by the Serbians and the closely allied former Yugoslavian National Army, significant numbers have been destroyed in tank-versus-tank battles and in bitter urban close-combat with both regular infantry and militia. Shoulder launched anti-tank weapons, ATGWs, 76 mm mountain guns, anti-tank guns and field artillery have all been used successfully against the M-84.

Specification:
First prototype: 1983
First production: 1984-current (over 650 built to date)
Current users: Croatia, Kuwait, Serbia, Slovenia, Former Yugoslavian National Army
Crew: 3
Combat weight: 41 000 kg
Ground pressure: n/av
Length gun forwards: 9.53 m
Width (without skirts): 3.37 m
Height (without AA gun): 2.19 m
Ground clearance: 0.47 m
Max. road speed: 60 km/h
Maximum range (with external tanks): 700 km
Fording: unprepared 1.2 m unprepared 5.5m

Gradient: 60%
Side slope: 40%
Trench: 2.8 m
Powerpack: multi-fuel V-46 V-12 diesel developing 780 hp and coupled to a manual transmission
Armament: (main) 1 x 125 mm gun (42 rounds); (coaxial) 1 x 7.62 mm MG; (anti-aircraft) 1 x 12.7 mm MG; (smoke dischargers) 12 single

Below: Former Yugoslavian Army M-84 MBT, the M-84 has proved to be particularly vulnerable to turret hits when in combat as these cause a catastrophic ammunition explosion that instantaneously kills the vehicle's crew and blows the complete turret off the vehicle.

Abbreviations

AA	anti-aircraft
ACV	Airborne Combat Vehicle (eg BMD family)
AEV	Armoured Engineer Vehicle
AFV	Armoured Fighting Vehicle
AIFV	Armoured Infantry Fighting Vehicle
AP	Armour Piercing
AP-T	Armour Piercing-Tracer
APC	Armour Personnel Carrier
APC-T	Armour Piercing Capped-Tracer
APDS	Armour Piercing, Discarding Sabot
APDS-T	Armour Piercing, Discarding Sabot-Tracer
APER-FRAG	Anti Personnel-Fragmentation
APERS-T	Anti Personnel-Tracer
APFSDS	Armour Piercing, fin Stabilised, Discarding Sabot
APFSDS-T	Armour Piercing, fin Stabilised, Discarding Sabot-Tracer
APHE	Armour Piercing, High Explosive
AP-T	Armour Piercing-Tracer
API-T	Armour Piercing, Incendiary-Tracer
AR/AAV	Armoured Recovery and Repair Vehicle
ARV	Armoured Recovery Vehicle
ATGW	Anti-Tank Guided Weapon
AVLB	Armoured Vehicle Launched Bridge
AVRE	Armoured Vehicle Royal Engineers
BARV	Beach Armoured Recovery Vehicle
BMY	Bowen-McLaughlin-York
CDC	Computing Devices Company
CET	Combat Engineering Tractor
CEV	Combat Engineer Vehicle
CFV	Cavalry Fighting Vehicle
CH AVRE	Chieftain Armoured Vehicle Royal Engineers
CHIP	Challenger Improvement Programme
CPMIEC	China Precision Machinery Import and Export Corporation
CRT	Cathode Ray Tube
DIVAD	Divisional Air Defense
ERA	Explosive Reactor Armour
FCS	Fire Control System
FST	Future Soviet Tank (American intelligence community designation usually suffixed by a number eg FST-1)
FV	Fighting Vehicle (British MoD designation usually suffixed by a number and version eg FV4030/4 - Fighting Vehicle 4030/version 4)
GPS	Gunner's Primary Sight
GPTTS	Gunner's Primary Tank Thermal Sight
HE	High Explosive
HE-APER-FRAG	High Explosive-Anti Personnel-Fragmentation
HE-FRAG	High Explosive-Fragmentation
HE-FS	High Explosive-Fin Stabilised
HE-T	High Explosive-Tracer
HEAT	High Explosive, Anti-Tank
HEAT-FS	High Explosive, Anti-Tank, Fin Stabilised
HEAT-MP-T	High Explosive, Anti-Tank-Multi Purpose-Tracer
HEAT-T	High Explosive, Anti-Tank Tracer
HEI	High Explosive, Incendiary
HEI-T	High Explosive, Incendiary-Tracer
HEP-T	High Explosive, Plastic Tracer
HESH	High Explosive, Squash Head
HESH-T	High Explosive, Squash Head-Tracer
HVAP-T	High Velocity Armour Piercing-Tracer
HVAPDS-T	High Velocity Armour Piercing, Discarding Sabot-Tracer
HVSS	Horizontal Volute Spring Suspension
IFCS	Improved Fire Control System
IFV	Infantry Fighting Vehicle
IR	Infra Red
LLLTV	Low Light Level Television
HESH	High Explosive, Squash Head
MBT	Main Battle Tank
MICV	Mechanised Infantry Combat Vehicle
MOLF	Modular Laser Fire Control
MRS	Multiple Rocket System
NATO	North Atlantic Treaty Organisation
NBC	Nuclear, Biological and Chemical
NORINCO	China North Industries Corporation
REME	Royal Electrical and Mechanical Engineers
RISE	Reliability Improved, Selected Equipment
SAM	Surface-to-Air Missile
SAPHEI	Semi-Armour Piercing, High Explosive, Incendiary
SAPHEI-T	Semi-Armour Piercing, High Explosive, Incendiary-Tracer
SCG	Self Changing Gears
SFCS	Simplified Fire Control System
SIRE	Sight Integrated Range Equipment
SMT	Soviet Medium Tank (Western intelligence community designation usually suffixed by M-date eg SMT M1990 - designation of T-72 M1990 before official Russian designation T-72BM became known)
STANAG	Standardisation Agreement (NATO)
TCM	Teledyne Continental Motors
TOGS	Thermal Observation and Gunnery Sight
TTS	Tank Thermal Sight
TWMP	Track Width Mine Plough
WarPac	Warsaw Pact
UAE	United Arab Emirates